Harnessing Innovation: Driving Change in a Digital Age

Embracing Technology for Business Success

Sarah Mitchell

Table of Contents

INTRODUCTION

Innovation ceased to be a luxury and became an obligation while living in this turbo-speed digital world. " Harnessing Innovation: Driving Change in a Digital Age: Embracing Technology for Business Success," looks at the transformative power of technology that defines the face of the future of business.

With companies struggling with the confusion of this digital age, adaptation has become almost the separating hallmark of either success or failure. It's about how leaders unleash innovations, harness emerging technologies, and build strategies that will surely drive, not just respond to change.

From truly understanding what innovation really means to the real application of a digital transformation strategy that really works, this book covers the complete road map necessary to thrive in an unmistakably digital business.

It shows the role of leadership, data-driven decision-making processes, and agility in coping with today's competitive environment. "Harnessing Innovation" shares practical insights through real-world case studies to equip readers to turn challenges into opportunities.

Whether business leaders in search of insight into the forces of change, entrepreneurs, or any inquisitive minds regarding the forces of change that continue to change the face of the business world today, this shall be your clear yet formidable guide to embracing innovation as the bedrock of your organization's success in the digital age. Your meaningful journey to change begins here.

CHAPTER I

Understanding Innovation in the Digital Age

The Evolution of Innovation

From the early stages of making tools to the advanced technologies of the digital age, innovation has always been an essential part of human development. Innovation grew from humanity's relentless pursuit of efficiency, further advancement, and discovery. Knowledge of this evolution will assist organizations in using innovation to navigate the future and provide insight into how societies have evolved over time.

The Evolution of Innovation

Innovation Sources	R & D	Vendors/ Suppliers	Users/ Customers	Crowd	Connected Products/Tools
Innovation Tools	Stage Gate	Open Innovation	Human Centered Design	Online Platforms	Artificial Intelligence Machine Learning

Innovation sprang from basic human needs for survival, shelter, and food. Working with the environment to their advantage, early humans fashioned tools and devised ways of gathering and hunting and defending themselves. As simple as these early acts may have been, they became the building blocks for further developments. Taming the elements of fire, the invention of the wheel, and the crude ways of agriculture were among the earliest major victories of human innovation. Combined, each development tended to enable increased productivity, higher standards of living, and greater control over the environment.

As the civilizations evolved, innovation tended to become more institutionalized, many times in response to problems associated with urbanization, trade, and governance. The ancient Greeks, Romans, and Egyptians made many fundamental contributions to such fields as engineering, mathematics, and medicine, to cite a few examples. The possibility of greatness of the human mind was manifested in inventions such as the construction of aqueducts, complex architectural designs, and inventions concerning navigation and measurement of time. Invention during this era very often sprouted out of the need to find workable and durable solutions to pressing problems.

During the Middle Ages, pragmatism and necessity were some of the most motivating factors behind invention. Although it was basically remembered as a time of little scientific progress, this century had been characterized by the numerous small-scale inventions that prepared the way for the Renaissance and beyond. Crop rotation, the heavy plow, and windmills were brought about by the agricultural revolution, which increased food output drastically. The longbow and walled castles were two military innovations that represented a need for strength and security. But even when the progress was slower, the preparatory work for further development had been done behind the scenes.

The 14th century ushered in the Renaissance, which accounted for a very significant era in the annals of invention. It was characterized by an inquisitive and exploratory spirit wherein there was a revival of interest in education, science, and the arts. The invention of the printing press by Johannes Gutenberg in the fifteenth century revolutionized knowledge dissemination by creating new means of expression and idea exchange. Navigation, astronomy, and medicine also saw dramatic improvements during this period, which set the stage for what would be subsequently referred to as the scientific revolution.

Perhaps the most pivotal milestone reached in innovation was the commencement of the Industrial Revolution in the late 1700s. It was characterized by the shift from rural, agrarian economies to an urban, industrialized society. Developments in metallurgy, mechanized textile production, and steam engine changed the means of producing and distributing commodities in quite radical ways. Mass production, factories, and developing new energy sources such as coal and then electricity characterized some of the developments in this era. Besides transforming economies, the Industrial Revolution changed social patterns, too, as people moved from the countryside to towns and cities in search of work.

The 20th century ushered in the modern era of invention, marked by extremely rapid technological innovation and radical changes in virtually all aspects of everyday life. The invention of the automobile, airplane, and telecommunications networks completely changed the way people related to the outside world and to each other. The world wars, horrible as they were, accelerated technological change in areas such as radar, computers, and medicine. Improvements in product design, marketing, and production helped drive the development of the consumer society in the years following the wars.

The Digital Revolution refers to the period when computers and Internet and other digital communication technologies became common; it dominated the latter half of the 20th century. What happened during that period was that the basic transition from analog to digital changed the way information would be handled, shared, and maintained. Just as the World Wide Web, in the 1990s, made it possible for people around the world to be connected to one another in ways hitherto unthinkable, the microprocessor of the 1970s made personal computing possible. The Digital Revolution was all about ways that governments, businesses, and people in general were influenced by the modern means of accessing information and finding new avenues for innovation in just about anything.

Innovation has continued into the twenty-first century with developments in industries like biotechnology, renewable energy, and artificial intelligence. Sometimes referred to as the Fourth Industrial Revolution, this era is characterized by the convergence of digital, biological, and physical technologies. Artificial Intelligence and machine learning have started changing many industries by automating tasks, enhancing decision-making capabilities, and developing new ways of interacting with technologies. The growth in the Internet of Things is integrating connection into common items, thus creating smarter homes, offices, and cities. These fields of study are in revolution in the development of genetically modified crops that can resist climate change through biotechnology and genetic engineering, and tailored medicines. The need to solve such global problems as resource scarcity and climate change, coupled with the drive toward sustainability, also pushes innovation in renewable energy, waste management, and sustainable practices. These days, it's more about solving major global challenges than it is about creating new products or services.

Another distinguishing feature of modern invention is its collaborative nature. Nowadays, all major discoveries are usually the result of an interdisciplinary collaboration and an international network. In contrast, invention in the past was seen, by and large, as a result of an isolated effort. At least three examples - the shared economy, crowdsourcing, and, finally, the open source movement - are cases of novel and unexpected ways in which collaboration boosts creativity. Businesses increasingly recognize that their success depends on multiple perspectives and are forming collaborative partnerships with higher education, other companies, and even competitors to spark creative breakthroughs.

The way in which innovation grows also reflects shifts in attitudes around failure and risk. Whereas innovation and exploration were very often abandoned out of fear of failure, today's fast-changing world increasingly sees failure as part of the necessary course of creativity. Failing fast" and "learning from mistakes" have become mantras in fields like technology and entrepreneurship. The transformation did indeed facilitate innovation in an agile manner, with quick prototyping, testing, and iteration possible.

The trajectory of invention indicates the fact that, in the future, change will, ostensibly, continue to be the sole constant. From social equity through to environmental sustainability, the 21st century will be fraught with many other challenges that need creative, innovative solutions imbued with inclusivity, ethics, and technology. One cannot overemphasize innovation into the future; it should be at the forefront in opening doors, enriching lives, and reinforcing a more just and sustainable society.

The road of invention is yet to be fully covered. Whenever there are new challenges, there will be more opportunities to invent. Innovation is a history of human ingenuity, tenacity, and the unrelenting pursuit of progress wherein every major breakthrough--from the simplest tools early humans fashioned to the modern complex technologies of today-was driven by innovation. Growth understood as such places this into a historical context and allows us to continue pushing the envelope of what is possible both in our personal lives and in the world, we exist within.

The Core Principles of Innovation

Innovation concerns the making of progress through new ideas, products, or processes whereby growth and change are achieved in any field. Innovation thus offers a way whereby organizations and society as a whole may solve problems, adapt to circumstances, and exploit opportunities. Whosoever desires to nurture an environment where innovation and thinking ahead of their time can thrive needs to hold an elementary understanding of how innovations actually do work. These are tenets that inventive undertakings are moored on to make them real feasible and relevant.

The clear vision and purpose stand right at the heart of what is called driving of ideas around creativity. Innovation should never be an end unto itself but be anchored by a higher aim or mission. The key point here is that innovation should have a focus, often enlightened by the needs it tries to fill or value it creates. A clear purpose sheds light upon creative efforts and helps resources and stakeholders rally towards one key objective. This sense of a purpose would drive meaningful and serious innovation to make sure efforts are not just original but relevant and useful in the target market.

The second underlying key principle of innovation is customer-centricity: an appropriate comprehension of the demands, problems, and preferences of clients is a common starting point of successful innovation. It is, in essence, the basic cornerstone of the underlying logic that places the client at the heart of the innovation process. Businesses seek to discover solutions for real needs and the improvement of customer experiences to develop products, services, and processes that can more personally touch their target market. It is this that forms the backbone of design thinking and user-centered design among other design methodologies, in encouraging makers to uncover needs, ideate solutions, prototype, and test in iteration. Moreover, such a strategy makes innovation more apt to be successful, with results more welcomed and valued by consumers.

The other core concept of innovation involves risk tolerance and leveraging from failure. By definition, innovation involves taking a risk and venturing into the unknown; by definition, both carry some potential to fail. The onus is turned around from positioning failure as some kind of retreat to an opportunity to have crucial learning. An innovative culture allows experimentation, considered risk-taking, and the agility to move fast. This approach, therefore, helps teams to try ideas frequently and makes them learn from mistakes continuously and often to improve. An enterprise that operates on this philosophy understands full well that not all ideas work, but the lessons learned from every setback may prove very important for future use. With this shift in mindset from one of fear of failure to an appreciation for it as a necessary part of the path to innovation, firms have the ability to be flexible and adaptable when confronted with problems.

The other important principle of innovation is the utilization of technology as an enabler. In the modern digital age, this smoothes out operations, enhances data analysis, and opens up new business avenues where technology acts as one of the main enablers for innovation. The idea is to leverage the newest technological advances for driving innovation initiatives. At the same time, technology shouldn't be treated as an end but as means for the materialization of more general ends of an innovation strategy. Firms that can manage technology in an effective manner at their innovation process enjoy improved productivity, new opportunities, and more value for clients. That is the direction in which the road to competitiveness goes in this space of innovation-being abreast with evolving technologies and their various uses.

Two other key ingredients that indeed support any successful invention are the elements of focus and simplicity. Being able to take that step back and simplify something down to its most basic form is truly an art form in a world that can overwhelm. And perhaps that is a key takeaway-things should not need to be overcomplicated; innovation should be clean and clear, with usability not overcomplicated by extraneous features. Indeed, many truly innovative solutions address issues in a forthright, understandable manner in such a way as to make them widely available and simple to use. It helps innovators avoid over-engineering or feature creep that detracts from the effectiveness of their ideas by keeping a razor-sharp focus on key features and functionalities that provide the most value. Resources and energy are also better off focused on the most promising ideas rather than being diffused across an extremely large base of companies.

Today, with a situation of growing turbulence and instability, the notion of resilience unravels. Innovation requires flexibility, readiness for changes, and strength to overcome obstacles which may appear on one's way. The analogy would insinuate that businesses and people have to be agile, able to change direction at any time, and survive the ups and downs associated with the innovation process. Building resilience into the process of innovation means creating structures and strategies that can absorb setbacks and keep the momentum of the innovation process when circumstances are less than perfect. It is this flexibility that forms the basis for long-term success and enables a business to stay not only relevant but responsive in a market that's in constant flux.

This should be underpinned, in the last resort, by the key principle of quantification of the impact and success. Innovation should be guided by clear metrics and key performance indicators that could help measure the results and progress. It's about benchmarking, monitoring key metrics, and recurrent analysis of the outcomes to make certain that innovation efforts are on track toward value delivery. The indicators that would actually be in use would depend on what the strategy of innovation is trying to achieve and include customer happiness, market penetration, revenue growth, or operational efficiency. By measuring impact, organizations can make informed, data-driven decisions, properly allocate resources, and iteratively enhance the strategy over time. The latter, in turn, would ensure that the 'Why' of innovation stays in tune with the imperatives of the business and continues to be an important contributor to business success.

In brief, some of the key ingredients for innovation would, therefore, include the concept of purposefulness, customer-centricity, risk-taking, collaboration, continuous improvement, integrability with technology, simplicity, flexibility, and measurement-all within a fairly detailed framework of thinking of and driving innovation. The following directives also reveal that innovation is something more than the simple creation of new ideas. Innovation means the realization of critical changes under added value. Organizations that adopt these kinds of principles can create a strong innovative culture that will support their success and development and, at the same time, prepare them to answer the challenges of the future. Basically, innovation is the finding of better solutions for problems; it is guided by these tenets.

Technology as a Catalyst for Change

Technology has played a historic role in industry restructuring, economic growth, and societal change. From the invention of the wheel to the dawn of the Internet, technology has served persistently as an agent of change, pushing the frontier of possibility and changing how we live, work, and interact with one another. In the modern-day digital era, technology adoption influences practically every sphere of human life. Understanding how technology acts as an agent of change will provide us with valuable lessons on the benefits and problems associated with it and also how people and organizations can turn technology to their advantage.

The biggest of these roles, perhaps, is pioneering innovation: technology advancement brings forth innovation, which often exposes new possibilities or avenues where this new technology can be used to create new products, services, or business models. For instance, the Internet brought about a revolution in information dissemination, commerce, and communication. It gave birth to social media, e-commerce, and so on, which fully transformed whole industries and consumers' behaviors. In like manner, today, advancements in areas such as artificial intelligence, machine learning, and data analytics act as the drivers for improvement in health care, the banking industry, and many others. These improvements provide services at the level of the individual, with enhancement in better decision-making and efficiency. It constantly feeds the innovation engine in making new ways of thinking and doing possible, thus helping firms and communities to cope with the conditions and demands that are always changing.

Moreover, technology also accelerates the pace of change with better means of communication and connectivity. Geographical boundaries once routinely hindered the exchange of ideas and information; technology has essentially removed those barriers. Mobile technology, high-speed internet, and digitally connected networks across the world have turned interdependence into an integral unit where information is conveyed within seconds of time over long distances. Such increased connectivity has enabled organizations to go global, operate with partners across boundaries, and access new markets-all things that have also entirely changed the aspect of personal communication. It has completely revolutionized the ways we work, learn, and get medical attention through telemedicine, online learning, and working remotely. Through this, technology acts as an active agent of change by knocking down the barriers, opening up new pathways to communication and collaboration.

Another critical way technology acts as an agent of change is in its abilities to amplify efficiency and productivity. Automation, artificial intelligence, and advanced software solutions have eased many processes in the industry. These save time and labor used to perform jobs and release human workers to think and act upon more strategic and creative work. Robotics and highly engineered machinery have transformed the manufacturing production lines in several industries, which come forth with the advantage of more output and lower costs. On the other hand, service sectors are benefited by means of technologies related to chatbots and automated customer service, which have helped improve customers' experiences through quicker responses while also eliminating any waiting times. The outcome in revenues will increase; furthermore, it will make firms more productive and innovative, which is helpful in improving growth. With technology improving day by day, the ease and efficiency it can bring out in procedures will keep on surfacing as the principal cause of change.

The second role that technology plays is that of an agent of change, whereby through it, knowledge and resources become available to one and all. In older times, access to opportunities, knowledge, and education was barred for many through social connections, economic standing, and geographic location. However, all this has changed with the new access technology has given to resources and knowledge; the playing field has been leveled. This has made it possible for anyone on the Internet to tap into the great reservoir of knowledge existing online. Online learning platforms present opportunities that once were only available to people who could attend an institution. With the advent of blockchain and decentralized finance, new conduits to financial services enable people to participate in the global economy and to do business free from traditional intermediaries, unwinding long-standing structures of power and authority. The democratization of access is a very powerful force of change: it empowers a person and their communities with the potential for self-agency, contributing to the economy in ways previously unimaginable.

It contributes significantly to solving some of the major problems being faced by earth these days, acting as an agent of change in the modern world. One leading problem that the entire world is facing nowadays is climate change for which technological variations are at leading edge to make mitigations easier and ensure more sustainability. Although the dependence on fossil fuels has become less acute, solar, wind, and hydroelectric power sources represent a part of our reduced greenhouse gas emissions. Energy storage, smart grids, and electric cars are under development to make such transition easier in a more environmentally friendly and sustainable energy system. Precision agriculture limits waste and makes better use of resources, while cultured meat, plant-based proteins, and other food technologies have the potential to provide sustainable alternatives to more traditional sources of nutrition. These, and so many more technical developments, have given us the capacity to solve some of the most critical environmental and social problems facing our world today.

Yet, as technology serves as an agent of change, there are disadvantages to be weighed assiduously. It is the rapidity of the rate at which technology changes that may be disruptive in the workforce to the extent that automation and artificial intelligence displace jobs while creating others for another type of set of skills. It is in this relationship that the essence of funding for education and training is given force, which will enable workers to adapt to the ever-changing character the labor market has taken. Furthermore, with digital technologies becoming integral to daily living, issues of data privacy, cybersecurity, and the ethical use of technology have increasingly become front-end concerns. However, this can be fully realized only when technology is applied correctly and its fruits are equitably distributed across society.

The second driver of change comes from how technology itself shapes the expectations and behavior of customers. Widespread ownership of smartphones, use of social media, and access to on-demand services have radically changed how consumers relate to companies, decide what to purchase, and expect service. The three Cs that the consumer of today is looking for are ease, individuality, and instant gratification. They're better informed, better connected, and more powerful than ever. These changes in customer needs have subsequently compelled the organizations to continuously develop and change strategies which would meet the changing needs of their customers. Business operations that do not embrace technology become outdated and lose their competitive advantage in the marketplace, where successful exploitation keeps them forward in front of competition, and sometimes opens unexpected opportunities.

In other words, technology is a powerful agent of change, engendering creativity and innovation, increasing collaboration and productivity, democratizing opportunities, and solving significant global challenges. Technology touches nearly every aspect of life-from business operations to how people relate to and communicate with each other and the natural environment. But for the power of technology to be properly harnessed, thoughtful and appropriate responses to the challenges it presents will be necessary. Embracing, thoughtfully, the promise of technology can help us employ its power in service of positive change and construct a future that is more sustainable, equitable, and prosperous for all. It is sure to be of utmost importance as its function evolves and shapes the ongoing evolution of our surroundings.

The Strategic Value of Innovation

More than just a buzzword, innovation has turned into one of the strategic resources enhancing success, competitiveness, and growth in a world time and again perceived as getting increasingly unpredictable and dynamic. Innovation principally draws much of its strategic value for all manners of businesses, governments, and organizations from its potential to create new opportunities, improve operating effectiveness, and keep abreast with an always shifting set of stakeholder and customer requirements and expectations. Embracing innovation as part of the core strategies may set them up to thrive, rather than just survive, in light of rapidly changing technologies, recasting market dynamics, and fiercely competitive global markets. In this respect, it is paramount for executives, in trying to meet such challenges and building strong, forward-looking organizations, to understand the strategic value of innovation.

Perhaps the most salient constituent of the strategic value of innovation is in its potential for creating competitive advantage. Innovation stands for that critical difference whereby the business enterprise can differentiate its particular goods or services from those of its competitors in today's high-speed marketplace, which can quickly commoditize such goods and services. Innovation-regularly offering new products, services, or business models-enables companies to open up new markets, tend to the emergent needs of their consumers, and strengthen their brand. Companies like Apple and Tesla would never have thrived if they did not innovate relentlessly with paradigm-shifting products that reset consumer expectations and set new standards for competitors. Innovation provides a competitive advantage to companies by helping them develop loyalty among their clients due to the fact that the latter become dependent on such peculiar goods and services.

Secondly, innovation is also important in achieving better profitability and growth. Innovation and discovery will allow businesses to find and exploit new sources of revenue that in turn will allow them to fund their growth. It would mean novelty in products, entering virgin markets, or smoothing out existing processes so that costs can be reduced and efficiency enhanced. The continuous innovation in cloud computing and logistics has grown Amazon far beyond its original e-commerce business to a powerhouse in other industries. In light of this, companies can save a lot by investing in innovation for improved business processes and productivity enhancement of their bottom line. Innovation thus proves to be a strong engine of growth that enables the companies to scale up with sustainability and meet the changed circumstances in the market.

The strategic value of innovation embraces its impact on resilience and risk management. Thus, the culture of innovation enables an organization to encounter factors of disruption and uncertainties in a world where change is the only constant. Innovation helps an enterprise take sharp turns and find new ways of servicing their consumers in cases of global crises like the COVID-19 epidemic, technology disruptions, or simply the altered taste of consumers. The proactive innovator is more usually agile and able to adapt, and thus face the problems rather than being out of sight, sideswiped. Just what happened with the pandemic: a good innovation foundation helped many organizations make fast adjustments in the models of service delivery, digital transformation, and remote work. This flexibility will not only help the business weather storms but will also put it in a position from where they will be able to avail themselves of the openings at moments when things may get chaotic.

Strategic innovation plays an important role in developing the culture of continuous learning and development. Innovation-oriented organizations often foster those aspects of culture that stress experimentation, creativity, and collaboration. Besides motivating the employees, such an innovative culture also appeals to the best talent that will relish being part of a firm pioneering progress. Such learning and improvement-oriented culture can help organizations be steps ahead by continuously bringing improvements in their processes, services, and products. A commitment to ongoing innovation means they are actually creating the future instead of merely reacting to changes within the marketplace. From Google to 3M, every company known for its innovative work environment gives their employees free will and the wherewithal to tinker, inspiring breakthrough products and services that create ongoing success.

On a strategic level, innovation can also create significant social impact and sustainable value. Innovation, in that sense, is one of the ways to give solutions in the long run not only for the benefit of the company but also for society in general, since this puts greater pressure on companies to devise ways of solving environmental and social problems for investors, customers, and government agencies. Innovations in sustainable value chains-such as waste management and renewable energy-contribute not only to environmental footprint reduction but also to new business opportunities in the emerging green goods and services market. Social innovations may also contribute to corporate reputation and enhanced stakeholder and community relationships through responses to societal concerns relating to, for example, inequality, health care, and education. Where companies employ innovation to link corporate goals with broader social goals, they are more likely to gain credibility, improve brand equity, and ultimately achieve success.

Innovation in improving the customer experience and engagement also appears to be of strategic importance. The consumers of today are so much more empowered, informed, and better networked than some time ago, and their expectations will continue to change rapidly. Innovation enables businesses to realize these aspirations-to create experiences that are more personal, useful, and frictionless. Innovative ways help businesses build more relevant and durable relationships with their customers. Certain examples could be leveraging data analytics to understand customer behavior much better or employing artificial intelligence for personalized suggestions. Continuously innovating in the customer experience, a company can create more satisfied customers, increase loyalty, and ensure lifetime value. Innovation capability in customer experience space could drive the strategic positioning of a company when it is often the key differentiator in today's era.

The notion of digital transformation goes in conjunction with the strategic importance of innovation. Companies embracing digital innovation are far better positioned to leverage new opportunities in search of competitive advantage, forcing strategic change as digital technologies continue to reshape the face of industries. Innovation can be considered to be one of the forces for digital transformation-business structuring, procedures, and consumer interaction reconceptualized from a technological point of view. Equipping the strategy with digital innovation empowers operations to be more effective and data-driven in their decisions, with new value propositions for the digitally conscious customer. A strategic focus on digital innovation differentiates the established company model and proves a source of immense value, as Netflix's novel deployment of technology in content delivery and personalized recommendations transformed the face of the entertainment industry.

Second, innovation is of strategic importance because it is capable of future-proofing companies. How one can foresee a trend that is about to emerge and arm oneself for it determines success in the rapidly changing world. Innovation can keep an organization competitive by trying new ideas, understanding emergent technology, and developing a strategy that keeps the organization current for the future. Apart from investment in R&D and industry trend watching, firms may foster innovation by providing a culture of inquiry and exploration that digs a wellspring of ideas for creative ideas that would serve them better tomorrow. Proactively being focused on innovation helps companies defeat the demons of today significantly, while also leveraging the opportunities that tomorrow may have in store.

Finally, there is a very strong connection between leadership and vision with the strategic value of innovation. Innovation really has to be driven from the top of the company if it is going to thrive. It follows that leaders who consider innovation as a strategic priority are most likely to invest in relevant resources, make their teams empowered to do what is necessary, and create a context where creativity and risk-taking flourish. The strategic leadership of innovation involves creating a compelling vision of the future, aligning innovation activities with organizational goals, and leading an environment that nurtures new ideas. Innovation can be a powerful success factor when inbuilt in the strategic objective of the organization and supported by a committed leadership team.

In other words, innovation applies to a multi-dimensional strategic scope impacting every area of organizational functions and their long-term strategies. Innovation has emerged as one of the critical drivers of success in a world that is increasingly complex and fast-moving. Innovation foments not just competitive advantage and growth but also resilience, sustainability, and customer centricity. Placing innovation at the heart of the strategy will provide an organization with the ability to ride uncertainty, leveraging newer opportunities and sculpting lucrative, future-proof, and influential success. The pace of change is quickening, and the capability for innovation will remain one of the major predictors of strategic and long-term organizational success.

Overcoming Barriers to Innovation

Indeed, innovation is considered a significant factor in enterprise growth and competitiveness for long-term success. It will enable the firm to avail itself of new opportunities that come along, changes within the marketplace, and the differing needs of their clients. Despite such acknowledged importance, however, too many firms apparently have problems trying to encourage an innovative culture and confront certain key obstacles to successful innovation. It is hoped that being aware of many issues keeping creativity from occurring as well as the possible remedies of how such remedies will pay off is done through the process of overcoming such obstacles. Obstacles to innovation are common, but the organization can become the fertilizing ground for innovation and radical change if learns to identify them and finds a way of overcoming the problem.

The greatest barrier to innovation is resistance to, or aversion to, change. This may become manifest at a number of levels within the organization, ranging from individual staff right up to the top management. Many people will instinctively prefer the status quo, particularly if the procedures and framework have proved successful in their previous operations. When people feel that the risks of innovation are greater than the benefits, a culture of complacency may set in. What this obstacle requires, however, is a change in corporate culture: experimentation-oriented, risk-taking, and mistake-learning attitudes. Here, leaders can really make a difference by painting a compelling vision of innovation, setting the tone for a flexible, open culture, and rewarding staff for embracing new ideas and challenging conventional wisdom.

One of the critical brakes to innovation is inspired by resource lack. Innovation tends to require money, time, and human capital. Considering that most organizations have restricted levels of resources, projects involved in innovation must compete with other priorities in the organization for access to resources. For the organizations to break through the barrier, they must perceive innovation investment as a strategic objective and not discretionary spending. This might include internal budget shifts to consider other avenues of funding, such as partnerships and venture capital, and even scheduling specific time for employees to devote to creative endeavors. Other ways businesses could make the most of resources available and reap better outputs are by forming a cross-functional innovation team that includes many levels of expertise and perspective.

The second most prevalent obstacle that renders one's innovation nil is organizational silos: departments that function autonomously and hardly with others. It always finds it cumbersome to conceptualize these ideas and set them up, where other divisions of the business are also involved. Silos may imply redundant work, lost opportunities to synergize, and a misalignment of strategic objectives. Breaking down these silos will require conscious efforts at fostering cooperation and communications within the organization. Cross-functional teams, promotion of information sharing, and putting in place collaborative tools and platforms may help bridge the departmental divides and forge an integrated approach to innovation. The leadership should also focus on a shared vision and group responsibility for innovation to make sure every single person in the company is pointed in the same direction.

Another critical obstacle to innovation may be a risk-averse culture. In most companies, it is emphasized to avoid failure. Such an environment may discourage employees from researching new ideas or bold ventures. This includes the risk-averse culture that may hinder creativity and lead to more incremental than revolutionary breakthroughs. The organization should develop an environment that views failure as a teaching tool and rewards reasonable risk when the threshold is to be crossed. This requires a climate of realistic expectations-that not all creative attempts will bear fruits but that the lessons from its failure can be carried forward in the next endeavors. Successes and lessons from failures could be celebrated, and the organizations should encourage employees to seek new opportunities without any penalty. Lack of Innovation Strategy: Each organization has to lay out a well-defined strategy with regard to innovation.

In the absence of any strategy on innovation, efforts will be scattered, unfocused, and misplaced in terms of their higher-order goals. The innovation strategy is a documented piece that describes the goals of an organization, priorities, and focus areas on innovation. This will ensure funding goes toward projects that have the most impact and allow innovation activities to be coordinated according to the general business plan. In developing an innovation strategy that indicates key sources of innovation, a business should take the lead. This may arise from the changes in the market or consumer wants or even from a technical breakthrough. A set of criteria has also to be laid down for rating and ranking ideas. It also requires the development of specific performance measures and periodic assessment and adjustment of the plan to reflect changes in the marketplace. Management and leadership practices at times act as a stumbling block toward innovation.

The top-bottom approach and hierarchical structures keep innovation within a boundary and bind the flow of new ideas across all sectors of business. The voice of workers might not be heard or they might not be free to experiment and be innovative. This barrier can be overcome if, instead, there are more inclusive and enabling management practices by the leadership, which create ownership and participation at every layer in the organization. This can be achieved by allowing freedom to try new ideas, by drawing staff members into the decision-making process, and by creating channels of bottom-up innovation-that is, recognizing and considering ideas coming from every part of the company. The leadership must also provide a model for innovative behavior in being open for new ideas, challenging the status quo, using risk-taking. Excessive fear of external competition may also inhibit innovation by firms as they will now become more concerned with answering competitors instead of concentrating on creative decisions they have to make and taking the lead.

This barrier may be surmounted when the organization seeks to engage regulators in a bid to understand how legislation is laid down to promote innovation. They shall take advice on how innovation can be done within the legal parameters at the moment and actually push toward the development of legislative frameworks that call for innovation. Organizations can confidently innovate in areas of investing in compliance knowledge through the development of internal capabilities, which are better positioned to negotiate the regulatory restrictions. Above all, the removal of obstacles to innovation holds the key for firms to thrive in today's competitive and fast-changing environment.

Most problems that get in the way of innovation-aversion to risk, organizational silos, scarcity of resources, aversion to change, absence of a clearly defined objective-have solutions that can be found and implemented through deliberate and mindful action. The organization can foster an enabling environment for creativity: it can reward experimentation and learning, tear down silos in the organization, empower employees, and integrate innovation initiatives with objectives and strategy. Besides, interaction with other stakeholders, such as customers, partners, and governments, might also be relevant in the solving by firms of some external problems and in the identification of new opportunities. Such barriers to innovation overcome, this requires a strategic process of embedding innovation at the core of organizations' operations and culture, active commitment from the top management leadership, and the ability to question the status quo. This would give businesses a great opportunity to exploit innovation to its fullest and provide the impetus for success and growth in the long run.

CHAPTER II

The Role of Leadership in Driving Innovation

The Innovator's Mindset

The innovative mindset is very critical in bringing success into today's fast and changing world. It can be manifested through various mindsets, precepts, and methods that finally enable innovation, trial and error, and continuous learning in individuals and institutions. This is one way of thinking that has been very instrumental in encouraging innovation, helping organizations cope with situations that are complex and involving change, and furthering the leverage for new opportunities. Understanding and building on this innovative mentality will make a huge difference in the capacity of a person to hurdle through various obstacles and drive significant growth in business, technology, education, and personal development.

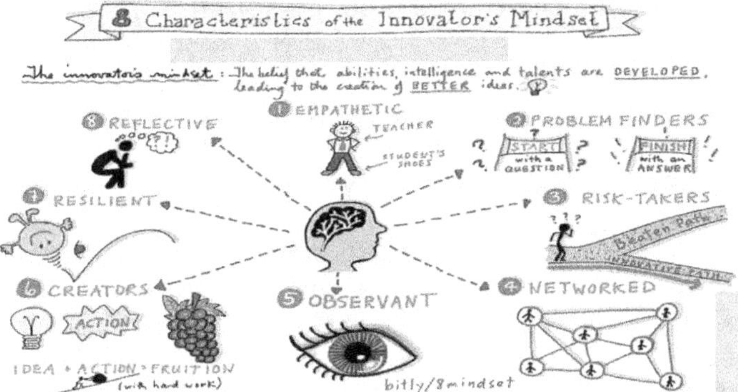

Innovative mentality at the core involves the tendency and knack for questioning established quos put on new lenses. That is, one question challenges the given practices, assumptions, and norms in a way that keeps one open to other ways of thinking. Innovators are never passively accepting whatever may come their way but are always on the lookout for new and different ways to enhance, modify, and transform the surrounding world. The innovator mindset also needs to know how things work and how they might be improved; thus, it demands a degree of inquisitiveness and a love of discovery. When an atmosphere of inquiry and critical thinking is developed in a body, they have the capability to invent new ideas and game-changing solutions. The next underlying ingredient to the innovator's thinking is resilience.

Innovation can be quite daunting and might therefore be difficult to handle where uncertainty and risks are concerned. People with the innovator's mindset look upon failure not as defeat but as learning and growing because they realize it is an inevitable part of the inventive process. Therefore, they would never yield to any challenge or defeat; rather, they consider every fall as an insightful input to a future endeavor. The talent of innovators to get stronger after each fall by continuing with the attempts to realize new ideas is crucial to maintaining momentum and inspiration in the face of adversity. Individuals and organizations can navigate more of the innovation process with greater personal ease by adopting a mindset that is both persistent and adaptable. The second principal underlying element of an innovator's mindset is creativity.

Creativity refers to the ability to come up with new and useful ideas, to combine seemingly paradoxical ideas, or to see problems from a new perspective. Innovative people are not constrained by conventional wisdom; they often draw their inspiration from diversified sources. They encourage experimentation, collaboration, and brainstorming in order to discover new ideas and solutions. Note that creativity is not solely the domain of artistic and design fields, but it is an enabling competence in problem-solving and strategic thinking across industries. In such an enabling environment that promotes innovation, creativity will multiply, hence distinction can be further fostered in any organization through a number of activities sharing ideas, collaboration across disciplines, and exploration. Other components of the innovator mindset include a strong sense of purpose and bias to power.

Innovators drive forward with the desire to solve big problems, to be in service of making an impact. Their purpose is to instigate change into organizations and communities through their ideas and solutions for the betterment of humanity. Goal-oriented motivation brings focus and determination to innovators. It allows them to push ahead even when they feel that their path is endless or filled with strife. Work is personally and organizationally relevant, innovative, and contributes to something greater than oneself when innovation efforts are aligned with a clear and inspiring purpose. Arguably the most important, collaboration is the second major part of the innovator's mindset.

Great innovation hardly ever comes out of one mind working in a vacuum but often is an end product of many minds working over and combining their thoughts and perspectives. Innovators are instinctively drawn to finding opportunities to connect with others, share, and collaborate since they inherently know that much more could be achieved with many minds put together rather than any one person could accomplish. They understand that this diversified thinking and the associated skills can lead to far deeper insights and more robust solutions. This co-operative technique generates a culture of free sharing and enhancement of ideas in an open, inclusive environment. Co-operative working puts organizations in a better position to exploit the various assets their teams own for enhanced innovation capabilities through the exploitation of offers that groups are able to solve. Taken together, these defining characteristics of the innovator's mindset reveal a commitment to life-long development and learning.

Innovators commit themselves for life to learn. They look for new experiences and information as sources of new talents and means to get ahead of the capacity curve. They seek opportunities for professional and personal growth, welcome feedback from others, and are anxious to learn from others. Innovators can be flexible, agile to changed conditions and new problems, offering creative responses due to their commitment to learning. This would ensure that the organization guarantees the competencies and expertise to drive continued innovation by cultivating a learning and development culture in the teams. In fact, it is an innovator's mindset that can be employed in all aspects of daily life and is not restricted in any way towards any field of operation or profession.

For instance, an innovator's attitude would bring into account teaching and learning in the classroom due to a certain mindset that would trigger or spark teachers and students to become challenge-accepting, adopt new ideas, and use technology where the practicality factor stands high. The innovator attitude will create the personal growth in terms of self-awareness, creativity, and strength that could give the right leverage to take control of one's life and make certain deterrence in incidents. With the innovator mentality, one could make all possible development, change, and influence that one deserves. Businesses need deliberate attempts and strategic methodologies for attitudinal change as an innovator.

Setting the tone and building an innovative culture are leadership tasks. They need to lead by example through acts of creativity, encourage experimentation, and create an environment where every staff member will be empowered to speak up and take risks. They can facilitate and enable innovation efforts through idea management systems, hackathons, and innovation labs. In a very real way, organizations can foster and develop innovation by providing the tools, support, and recognition for ideas that are creative. Finally, the innovator's mindset is certainly one of the most powerful and game-changing processes involved in building impact, adaptability, and innovation.

The adoption of resilience, creativity, curiosity, determination, cooperation, and continuous learning forms the foundation that both the individual and organizations need to develop to nurture and promote innovation and substantive change. It takes courage and calculated risk to change things; it takes collaboration, and above all, the innovations an organization can create will define its very long-term success. An innovative attitude of a innovator develops when there is a creative culture, along with a set of tools and resources which would bring new ideas into being. Success will demand the innovator mindset, and this will be a positive stimulus for those people desiring to change the world inside and outside their professions as the pace of change accelerates.

Building a Culture of Innovation

This culture establishment of innovativeness plays a significant role in enabling organizations to be successful through continuous change in the business environment and to be competitive. It espouses a culture of innovations, striving for new ideas, and enhancing without end. Such an innovative culture coupled with the stimulation of product and service innovation will further enhance the ability of an organization to adapt itself to changing circumstances, surmount various challenges, and surf emerging opportunities. What is needed to build an innovative culture is a multi-dimensional approach where creativity-stimulating techniques are combined with leadership commitment and allow experiments and out-of-the-box thinking.

The most critical element in forming an innovative culture is the leadership commitment. The leaders outline the values of the organization besides setting the standards for the importance of innovation. It is then left to the leaders to promote and exhibit innovative behavior by putting into practice their inventiveness and risk. Business-centered R&D is reinforced through project financing and publicly reinforcing ideas with passion on innovation. An experiment culture may also be nursed, which affords staff opportunities to try out new concepts, as well as make suggestions for improvements without penalty. The first requirement for this is the acceptance of a different mindset-one that embraces change and is focused on continuous improvement rather than the status quo.

Along with strong leadership, the enabling organizational structure holds the key to building an innovative culture. In some cases, traditional hierarchical organization gets in the way of creativity because these hierarchies tend to raise the barriers to cooperation and communication. This can be overcome by the organizations through more adaptive and collaborative structures that enable free flow of ideas and cross-functional collaboration. This would be manifested through the setup of ideas management systems, innovation laboratories, and frequent brainstorming sessions that allow employees across many departments to come together and discuss ideas or work on creative projects. It breaks down the silos that prevent innovative, multi-disciplinary collaborations across diverse perspectives and experiences that fuel actionable creativity in pragmatic solutions.

In other words, creating an innovative culture is providing workers with the materials they need to think up and actualize ideas. It includes financing education programs that would increase the capacity of employees to think outside of the box, solve problems analytically, and perform project management. This can also include dedicated time and resources for innovation projects provided to organizations, such that employees can take some time to look for new ideas and experiment with approaches that may be innovative. These are enabled in a number of different ways, such as offering funding towards specific research projects, staff access to innovative technologies, and innovation hubs where staff can seek support and mentorship. With such an approach, organizations cultivate an innovative culture in which taking the risk to turn one's creative ideas into reality allows success to become more likely to follow.

The other core constituent of the creative culture is fostering a continuous learning improvement culture. The employer has to facilitate an environment that will motivate employees to learn from both success and failures. It requires an understanding and acceptance of the fact that failure forms part of the circle of innovation, and not all creative ideas bear instantaneous fruits. This, in turn, is a call to intentionally create a learning culture where experimentation and learning from attempts at change that fail would be appreciated by managers and leadership. Reframing failure as an opportunity for extreme learning, rather than defeat, will help the employer build a progressive and resilient mindset among the employees. They can also be encouraged toward continuous professional development and staying current with changing technology and industry developments that may help them be creative and flexible within an environment of rapid change.

Incentivizing and Recognizing Catalyzes Innovation Culture. Organizations should provide a system where the creative contribution from individual and group levels is applauded and recognized, respectively. It can be through prizes, formal schemes of recognizing excellence, or even public acknowledgement of innovative projects. Recognition and rewarding creative initiatives are ways of encouraging workers to try new ideas while highlighting innovation as something very important to the firm. It is crucial that incentives and recognition programs be in concert with the belief and objectives of the organization and that their intent be to facilitate teamwork and group achievement and not individual competition.

The encouragement of experimentation and risk taking is another characteristic of an innovative culture. An environment where workers feel psychologically safe, experimenting and taking risks would not make them afraid of being either rejected or failing. A company can only help promote open communication, constructive criticism, and a friendly atmosphere that makes the workers feel important and valued as employees. It also allows the practices that enable fast prototyping and iterative development to facilitate low-risk testing and refinement of ideas by the staff. If an organization gets an iterative improvement process and embraces a try-and-fail approach, then the probability of success may go high.

A well-defined and exciting vision is in congruence with general strategic objectives of the organization that helps the innovative culture. It is the job of the leaders to inspire with a vision that motivates and inspires staff and gives direction and purpose to the staff's creative efforts. The mission and values of an organization should be wrapped into its vision through effective communication. When innovation projects are in line with more general strategic objectives, organizations can not only make sure that their efforts in innovation will focus on areas of great impact that hence contribute to the attainment of long-term successful results but also the innovation-objectives alignment could enable them to perceive their contribution to the overall scheme of things and hence lead to greater employee commitment toward innovative organizational objectives.

Apart from that, an organization should try to solicit and integrate the views and opinions of various partners, employees, and customers. One can utilize valuable opinions and views from external stakeholders in order to create and build innovation through interaction. Customers' feedback guides new products and services development; it also enables one to detect unsupplied needs. It may also be open to new insights and competencies from other players, such as startups, universities, or industry associations. By creating feedback channels for collaboration, the organizations can keep their finger on the pulse of the latest opportunities and trends in the industry and be assured that meaningfulness and relevance are created for their innovation work.

Building a strong innovation management system is part of establishing an innovative culture. It is the development of processes and structures to manage creative ideas, initiatives, and projects. Examples are mechanisms of project selection, resource allocation, idea generation, and performance evaluation. Management of innovation should be in a systematic organization to ensure that activities related to innovation are transparent and well-organized. Activities are directed towards the strategic objectives. An innovative management system may also serve to monitor the development, measure the success, and determine further needs of development with which companies can strive and refine their continuous innovative activities.

In other words, building up an innovative culture is a pervasive and strategic process that requires not just leadership commitment but resource allocation, continuous learning, risk-taking, vision, contact with stakeholders, and good management. It can also be said that an organization will have a dynamic and robust culture; it will be innovative-expanding when the atmosphere in an organization inspires experimentation, creativity, and ideation. Great innovation cultures possess strengths beyond projects or initiatives in that sense, as they develop an organization's capabilities for long-term success, adaptability, and competitive advantage. An innovative culture has been, is, and will be essential to continued success and to fully harness the numerous opportunities and challenges provided by the fast-moving pace of change.

Navigating Change Management

This is one of the most important competencies that help an organization embrace and employ new strategies in response to market demand for its products, exploring avenues of dealing with the surroundings that are time to time changing. The change element, considering relevant driving factors such as changing technology, consumer behavior, updated regulations, and intense competition, is unconquerable in today's world. Effective change management applies not only to the actual rollout of new procedures or systems but also to facilitating and developing change within the staff members themselves, which helps take care of the human side of that particular change. Where the organization manages that change well, it is competent enough to attain its goals with minimum disruption and maintain employee engagement along with morale.

Great and inspiring is the vision that should accompany effective change management by nature. The leaders must be in a position to expound on the justification for the change in case it is necessary and if it falls within the strategic direction of the organization. This communication of vision as either partners, customers, or employees with all participants involved must be constant and vivid. A good vision makes it clearer for the people what exactly to expect from the change and how it is going to affect the jobs and responsibilities of the people. Thirdly, good communication may include a voice of concern and questions that may pop up, making sure everybody is informed and on board with the goals of the change.

The second most important element of the described process is preparing the organization for change. This involves planning as a way of evaluating the current status imitating the possible impacts of the change, and designing a proper plan regarding implementation. In fact, the detailed impact assessment helps an organization understand through which areas the change would take place what kind of obstacles may exist there, or what the resistance is. The things on which assessment needs to be considered vary from organizational structure to procedures, technology, and culture. In turn, this may become the basis for a more detailed change management plan by organizations, articulating specific step-by-step steps that need to be taken toward expected results, timelines for that, resources to be deployed, and mitigation plans against the associated risks.

One of the most critical aspects of change management relates to workforce engagement because, very often, they lead the change. Hence, support from their side and commitment become of prime importance to bring success to any change. Participation is achieved by involving employees in the process of transformation right from the very beginning, which consists of seeking views from them, listening to and addressing their concerns, and then incorporating them into a strategy for change management. In addition, giving employees a greater say in decisions and involving them in implementing change usually increases commitment and ownership of change.

The organizations, in turn, prepare the staff through training and support so that they can keep on developing the necessary skills and knowledge for new procedures or systems. This will help them to create supportive environments that will ease the transition through active participation and listening to employee concerns.

Leading the Organization through Successful Change Management An organization might lead its workers through successful change management if the leaders are in a position to portray, through ideal examples of wanted behaviors and provision of support for the change, the commitment of the organization to the change process. By this, it means that the lines of communication are not closed; rather, the approaches are one-on-one, visible, and active concerning problem-solving. During the implementation process for the change, leaders should be ready to act as problem solvers on how they will handle disagreements and also to surmount the resistance factor:. The leaders may create a trust-based environment and facilitate the staff to respond to the change by portraying themselves resistant yet confident.". Let the milestones and achievements be identified by the leaders themselves only so as to keep the ball rolling and focus on the positives of the change.

Resistance to change many times has been an issue of any organization in the process of change management. This resistance may be due to a variety of reasons. Common ones include discomfort with new ways of working, job security concerns, and fear of the unknown. In this direction, an organization needs to adopt a proactive approach toward handling resistance through the early establishment of sources of resistance and the developing of mitigation techniques. This can be through the availability of support and reassurance, addressing specific issues through selective engagement and communication campaigns. Resistance can also be overcome, and more support is offered through the engagement of key influencers and promoters of change within the organization. When organizations appreciate and resolve the original cause of resistance, they are able to establish a better attitude towards change and hence improve the success of the implementation.

Monitoring and review of the progress give the necessary adjustment on the path to the effective accomplishment of desired changes in projects for change. The precise identification of metrics and performance indicators will facilitate the monitoring of organizations regarding how effective the initiatives of transformation are. It will involve constant evaluation concerns about the state of affairs in terms of pre-set goals and objectives, contributions, and views of members of staff and other stakeholders. The identification of areas that require development will also be involved. The monitoring should be a continuous process so that the business decisions are based on evidence and the strategies can be changed as per needs. This is because, through this, organizations are able to build their capacity to realize intended results along with long-term success since they are in a position to know about the effects of the change and be responsive to emerging new concerns.

The second important factor in managing change is the issue of creating a supportive culture of change. General resilience can be elicited with respect to an organization, and transitions can be so smoothly wrought by building a culture that retains the hallmarks of innovation, adaptation, and continuous learning. The attitude will be one that can be fostered in meeting change, not as any form of threat, but as an opportunity toward growth. A culture that encourages collaboration and effective communication and enables opportunities for professional development-all results in an environment that embraces change and supports staff through change. The supportive approach of organizational culture toward the goals of change means when these are imbibed into the working culture, organizations would be able to cope with changes more effectively to bring about continued success.

Apart from the internal change management components, organizations have to consider the external factors that will influence their respective change effort. It is here where knowing one's market, recent legislative changes and competitive pressures in terms of possible impacts on the change effort comes into relevance. Knowing how companies interact with external partners, suppliers, and consumers may provide them with greater understanding and insight to align the change initiatives with general market trends and expectations. An allowance of external factors to flow into the change management process will allow organizations to update and flex their plans toward changing business conditions.

In other words, change management takes work; it is inevitable for growth and adaptation to the ever-changing environment. This shall be done through a range of actions comprising setting the vision, strategy, and plans for the change, providing the preparation and enabling employees to function within the new environment, exercising effective leadership itself, handling resistance, and monitoring progress. Other influencing factors include establishing a supportive culture and the consideration of external factors, too. This would help the organizations in issuing strategic and holistic approaches towards change with increased capacities in the delivery of new initiatives with the attainment of goals while supporting the competitive advantage. Since this feature of the business world will not be going away anytime soon, competency in managing such change will be increasingly necessary to enable organizations to maintain ongoing success and viability.

Empowering Teams to Innovate

Therefore, self-managed teams should be absolutely free to innovate if they are to be competitive and adaptable to ever-changing markets. Today, innovation needs to be across the breadth and width of the organization, not in the hands of a few leaders or some R&D department. It is only when organizations create a culture of experimentation, autonomy, and collaboration that creative potential gets translated for teams. Empowerment for innovative teams is more than just equipping the teams with tools and resources to become innovative; it actually denotes a paradigm shift in the way teams are identified, supported, and stitched into the wider innovation strategy of the organization.

Underpinning empowering teams is the concept of autonomy. Most energized and inspired people are when left to experiment and conduct their ideas. The power of autonomy will enable the team members to take ownership through choices and innovative approaches. Ownership does more than motivate people; it actually encourages them to think out of the box and take calculated risks. This will help the teams within an organization by facilitating their autonomy in terms of setting expectations and goals while giving latitude in the choice of ways for effective achievement of those goals. It is here that a balance between guidance and autonomy should be helpful in effective team innovation.

The other main component will involve nurturing the teams with the required resources and tools. Innovation is allowed by resources such as information, tools, and technology accelerators that enable the creation and testing of novel ideas. For example, one can only assume that investments in infrastructures and mechanisms-such as advanced technology, R&D centers, and access to relevant information and market insights on which innovative efforts will depend are justified. Teams should also be granted sufficient time to devote to work on creative projects, including blocked-out times for ideation, prototyping, and testing. In this way, organizations create space for innovation by giving teams the time and resources.

The second key ingredient in creating team empowerment is collaboration. Rarely does innovation take place within the vacuum of an individual. As a matter of fact, most innovations are brought about normally through combined effort contributed by people with distinctively different experiences and perceptions. Shared ideas, more creative business solutions, and many more bottom-line business outcomes from collaboration among teams and inside of teams bring many results. Companies allow collaboration to take place by creating space and providing opportunities for various members of their teams to meet, share ideas, and work toward different projects. This can be in the form of teams across functions, brainstorming sessions, or collaboration platforms and technologies. Breaking down silos in organizations to enable collaboration, therefore, unleashes the cumulative genius of the groups involved while fostering an innovation process.

It means the team enables experimentation for innovation. Innovation means trying out ideas and ways for the first time, which naturally carries a hint of risk with it. It allows space to try new things and test concepts without perceived negative consequences of the outcome. The equation needs to be flipped from failure avoidance into learning from failure to enable the experimentation culture. Organizing teams should learn to regard failures as opportunities to learn and advance rather than as some retribution. It is this thinking that underlies two increasingly important aspects in the development of creativity: risk and resilience. The experimentation should, therefore, be emphasized with recognition and celebrations even if immediate success may not come forth, which again would further stress the value of the approach and motivate the groups to continue trying new things.

Encouraging innovation from teams requires inspirational leadership. Leaders also need to demonstrate the attitudes and behaviours that they wish to see in their teams if innovation is to be encouraged and supported-open-mindedness to new ideas, constructive feedback, and the willingness to take calculated risks. Then again, it is also very important that the teams be able to draw on effective leaders, so as to help surmount the challenges and eliminate any obstacles which may confront them as a result of innovating. That is to say, leaders create a context in which teams feel highly motivated and confident in their potential to innovate by giving them guidance, tools, and encouragement. In return, leaders will seek out thoughts and opinions from their teams so that they feel valued and heard as part of a decision-making process.

Systems of rewards and recognition ensure that an innovative culture is sustained. Team achievement can be recognized to lift morale, motivation, persistence, and participation in creative efforts. Rewards may be formal: rewards, bonuses, but also less formal: acknowledgement, praise. Where innovation involves the organization's very principles and objectives, they should be translated into its recognition and award scheme. What it means is that effort, creativity, and risks during the process of innovation should be recognized rather than the successful process alone. Matters of praise or recognition for creative achievement could also entice a sense of the importance of innovation and encourage further innovation of new ideas by teams.

Innovation empowerment will be necessitated through training and development, which may provide knowledge and tools to team members to support creativity and feeling empowered to act effectively and confidently. Examples include problem-solving techniques, project management, innovative use of technology, and creative thinking. Organizations also need to contribute to their employees' continuous learning and professional growth so that they can keep abreast of what happens on the market with regard to state-of-the-art practices. Investing in teams helps the firm to have a knowledgeable workforce fully packed with talented ideas that are innovatively put into action. Iteration and feedback form the two most important parts of the innovation cycle.

In fact, timely and constructive feedback might be due in time to develop ideas and methods. These would involve stakeholders, customers, and colleagues. Iterative processes-in other words, trying ideas, testing them, getting feedback, and then iterating- may be the best way to make innovative solutions more robust and effective. This will mean creating ways of gathering and using input throughout the innovation process and placing organizations in a position whereby teams would be placed at positions where they need to know to make savvy decisions and adjustments. The other empowering approach through which teams can innovate is by creating a psychologically safe work environment.

It's an environment where its members should find themselves safe enough to point out, say, and ask about flaws in current processes without condemnation or backlash. Opening up the door to open communication and collaboration, positive psychological safety allows your teams to do new things-even take risks. Positive psychological safety is bred from inclusive, respectful, and supportive cultures. That means leaders themselves have to model and facilitate the behaviors of active listening, giving constructive feedback, and empathy-safety in the environment. In other words, enabling teams to innovate is multi-layered: done in an enabling environment that provides for autonomy, development, tools, and support, facilitates collaboration, and fosters building an experimentation culture.

Leadership, recognition, and training will also support innovative initiatives and team engagement. By paying attention to these key components, an innovative climate unleashes the creative power in teams that brings great improvements. With the accelerating change in the world, encouraging innovation in teams becomes vital for long-term success, necessary to maintain competitive advantage in an ever-changing business world.

Measuring Leadership Impact on Innovation

The level of innovation by the leaders of the organization should be measured by showing how they could influence creative processes and outcomes that occur within their teams. Indeed, effective leadership may strongly drive innovation through elements like a positive work atmosphere, clear goals set, and autonomy given to staff. However, measurement of such influence must be done based on how it affects innovation activities and their results directly and indirectly. Understanding and quantifying this impact is, therefore, critical to ensure that innovation initiatives align with corporate objectives and that the strategies of leadership are optimized. One of the keyways leaders influence innovation involves establishing and maintaining a culture that fosters and celebrates creativity. Innovation leaders-that is, those leaders who place a high emphasis on innovation-offer an enabling environment for experimentation and new ideas. It can be quantified by various feedback mechanisms, engagement metrics, and employee surveys, to name a few. For example, the surveys can also look forward to how open and open-minded the culture of the company is towards new ideas and how it stands in support of taking risks and trying new experiments. The level of involvement in events and projects dealing with innovation-related matters may also reveal the extent to which innovation culture has been assimilated. Such spheres show where an organization can assess a leader's competency in embedding innovation culture.

The strategic direction and vision of the leaders are another significant determinant of innovation:. One of the main tasks of a leader is to define what strategic priorities and goals for innovations are, and to set them in correspondence with the general organizational objectives. The relevance and clarity of this strategic guideline may be measured, for example, by the relevance of projects dealing with innovations to the goals of an organization. Innovation-oriented KPIs, such as the number of new developed services or products, revenues generated with respect to these innovations, and increase of market share, may provide information on how well leadership vision has materialized. Thirdly, assessment of how effectively the strategy of innovation is communicated and integrated into daily work will help measure how effectively leaders guide their people toward innovative goals. Two key elements of leadership that influence creativity deal with support and empowerment. When leaders are better able to enable their teams through resources, training, and autonomy, the outcomes are more effective innovations. The impact can be measured by assessing the level of funding and support to innovation initiatives, how empowered staff is to explore and execute their ideas. Indicators of how the leaders encourage innovation would be metrics around training programs available, team autonomy, and availability of technology and tools. Additionally, employee feedback and satisfaction surveys provide insight into how empowered people feel and if they believe their leaders would support them in pursuing new ideas.

Another source of measurement for how well a leader fosters innovation is the level at which resistance to change is managed and overcome. Usually, innovation requires new procedures, different tools, or methods of operation that are resisted by staff members. Such leadership can handle and lead their fellow workers to change at innovation. In fact, the measurement would include how effective the change management techniques put in place would be and the capability of the leaders in handling and overcoming resistance. This would be achieved through surveys measuring attitude about change, remarks regarding the change management process, and what percentage of innovation efforts are successful. Organizations can also find out how leaders are showing change facilitation by managing resistance to change and clearing the way for easier transitions. Innovation requires collaboration and teaming. Leader influence in these areas is a function of how the leaders manage and facilitate team interaction. Leaders that create a collaborative environment and cross-functional teams bring together people with different viewpoints and hence enhance the creative process. This benefit also involves quantification by assessing the collaboration among teams and departments. This builds a culture of collaboration that can be measured with metrics related to the frequency and success of cross-functional initiatives, effective collaboration and communication, and extent to which multiple teams have engaged in innovation activities. In addition, the effectiveness of leadership intention to team up and collaborate may also be found through assessment from project outcome and feedback from the members of a team.

Besides these direct measurements, the effect of leadership on creativity needs also to be put into a broader organizational perspective. This would involve assessing an organization's competence to realize its innovation goals and the general project outcomes on innovation. Good measures could include the number of patent applications, success rates of new product launches, and return on investment realized from innovation efforts. It is also benchmarked against industry standards and best practices, hence giving firms complementary ways of gaining insight into how well a leader drives innovation by comparing performance against that of their competitors and highlighting areas where improvement needs to be made.

Succession planning and leadership development also form part of the measurement in the impact of leadership on innovation. Long-term success will depend upon the output of the leaders in the future who can drive innovation. Succession planning procedures and reviews of effectiveness of leadership development initiatives underpin how effectively companies are training executives to drive and support innovation. Examples are how effectively leadership development programs better equip heirs with jobs associated with innovation, and how leadership competencies match innovation objectives. In any case, it is the feedback and continuous development that matter most when looking at how leadership can affect innovation. With active solicitation of input and a commitment to development, leaders can be much better at fostering innovation. This dimension of measurement will have an impact on how leaders institute feedback into their practices of leadership, how many tactics are changed based upon the input provided, and what the overall effect will be on improved innovative outcomes. Feedback mechanisms, performance appraisals, and studies relating to leadership efficacy may identify how leaders are improving their approaches to fostering innovation over time.

CHAPTER III

Leveraging Technology for Business Success

Identifying Key Technologies

Identification of the critical technologies is indispensable for any organization interested in the enhancement of innovation, gaining a competitive advantage, and meeting strategic objectives. Long-term success in this fast-moving technological world has come to be based on an ability of organizations to anticipate those few innovations that will make significant impacts. The process involves interpretation of new trends, evaluation of technological capabilities, and integration of such tools with the objectives of the corporation. Identification and proper exploitation of key technologies can enable a firm to respond to changes in the marketplace, achieve leadership, and generally improve performance.

Key technologies are selected starting from a general knowledge of new trends and technical developments. The technology today is changing faster than ever. New developments on the road to change in the markets open up new career opportunities. A competitive organization has to be informed about recent developments in areas of high relevance for the future, including artificial intelligence, blockchain, cloud computing, Internet of Things, and cybersecurity. Means that effectively find out about new and developing technologies are monitoring of trade journals, technology conferences, and influential people. By monitoring trade journals, attending technology conferences and talking to key individuals, the organizations can help ensure they know the new and developing technologies emerging with some probability of causing revolutionary effects either within an industry or to business processes. Rating Each Technology in View of Its Benefits, Risks and Technological Readiness is the further stage of a new technologies estimation regarding their probable impact and enterprise utility. That is, the organizations will want to consider issues such as scalability of the technology, interoperability with existing systems, and maturity. Maybe an emergent technology holds great promise for the future but simply is not ready for wide-scale adoption today. Conversely, in respect, a mature and proven technology with demonstrated benefits is much better positioned to be quickly adopted. It's through such variable analyses that organizations can identify those technologies that create maximum possibility and, hence, align with their strategic goals.

The other two important factors involve identifying the technologies that are required and finding out how they compare against the strategic goals and objectives of the organization. Besides technical capabilities, technologies must also be scanned for their appropriateness toward the greater vision and mission of an organization. For example, advanced analytics and machine learning powering personalized experiences are relevant if the strategy of a company is to improve customer experience. In such cases, spending focused on strategies makes technology investments focused on business growth and competitive differentiation. Alignment makes for the right decisions on which technologies to adopt, invest in, or build. Identification of the important technologies considers competitive environments and market dynamics. This will help in depicting opportunities as well as risks by learning the ways rivals use technology. While analyzing the technology strategy of competitors, organizations can find their gaps in technological capability and study ways to differentiate themselves. The competitive analysis would be based on scanning the rivals' collaborations, product offerings, and technological investments. The interaction with industry analysts and consulting organizations brings a wide view of technological trends and competitive positioning. This enables a company to stay in step with changes in the competitive environment and provide the information necessary to drive decisions about strategic investments in technologies, thus determining how best to posture for competitive advantage.

The identification of key technologies obviously involves considerations of potential return on investment. These are trade-offs that an organization has to consider between the implementation of new technologies or investing in them and benefits that accrue from the same, keeping in view financial implications regarding costs of implementation, maintenance, and likely accruable benefits. It is important in doing a full study of the return on investment to estimate other revenues, savings of costs, and other gains in efficiency one could expect from use of technology. The study must be duly considered for various risks and uncertainties that might be associated with the technology. The determination of the return on investment would stipulate the ways an organization views the technology as a potential investment that would align investment priorities. Apart from financial implications, there are operational and technological implications when organizations bring about new technologies. This will be in understanding how the technology aligns with pre-existing systems, the effect the technology has on company procedures and processes, and how much change management is required. Those technologies that demand great changes to existing systems or processes are likely to be difficult to implement and far-reaching in their implementation. Any such technologies, were they to have serious impact, would demand very serious resource allocation and planning. Although technologies that best fit within the system of pre-existing processes and procedures may have easier adoption and a faster realization of benefits, the understanding of such practical implications helps the business to anticipate challenges and develop an effective strategy toward adoption of the technology.

Organizational readiness for change is another critical variable in identifying the key technologies. In so many ways, the successful adoption of new technologies is often prefaced by the ability of the organization to cope with change effectively. It would also include assessment with regard to the culture of the organization, leadership support, and availability of knowledge and experience. Ensuring that the workers function with emerging technologies will require a commitment from the organizations to invest in training and development. Equally important would be overcoming the resistance to change and developing a culture to adopt innovation and change to ensure successful adoption of technology. It can also locate the impediments likely to occur at the organizational level and plan strategies for overcoming these. Besides this, strategic alliances and collaboration can also play a key role in locating and utilizing the crucial technologies. In cooperation with technology suppliers, academic institutions, and business partners, resources, knowledge, and new technologies would be available. It could also provide an opportunity to pilot new technologies and enable the company to update its knowledge on new innovations, as well as the process of innovation itself. As a result, the capacity of an organization to adopt and implement innovations through joint ventures and strategic alliances would increase accordingly. This is with regard to the fact that through the exploitation of external linkages, organizations may come across relevant information and resources which are necessary to support their technological plans.

Finally, it can never be overemphasized that business firms should continuously assess and recheck their technological plans. With each passing day, the world of technology continues to change, and any new development may prove to affect those technologies that have already been set. The possible ways through which flexibility can be attained by firms in changing direction, if need be, lie in reevaluation of strategic objectives, monitoring of the effectiveness of the implemented technologies, and periodic analyses of emergent trends in technology. This constant review will keep the technology plans fresh and relevant according to the dynamic goals and requirements of the enterprise. Put differently, identification of critical technology is broad activities comprising operational and organization implications, competitive analysis, technological capability assessment, alignment of technology with the strategic objectives of the organization and understanding the emerging trends. Correct identification and implementation of the critical technology build an organization's competitive advantage, innovation, and realization of strategic objectives. The race of the continuously developing technical environment does not allow anything else but constant re-evaluation and readjustment if one wants to stay ahead of events. Only if the organization carefully estimates the potential of the critical technologies and strategically prepares for them, can long-term success and leading positions be reached in the respective industry.

Digital Transformation Strategies

Success consists of the road to developing a digital transformation strategy that enables the organization to win in this digital world. A business has to be ready for a change at the unprecedented rate at which technological advancements are made in its effort to sustain competitiveness, achieve better consumer experience, and enhance operational efficiency. The successful digital transformation plan has a multi-dimensional approach: process re-engineering, technology adoption, and cultural transformation. The transformation in operations, business models, and state-of-the-art engagement with customers through the effective use of digital tools and technologies will henceforth yield major dividends for the organization in terms of performance and agility. Any successful strategy for digital transformation requires a sound and capable vision. It needs to outline how digital technologies will be leveraged in solving critical business problems and in achieving strategic objectives. It involves the analysis of the existing status of a group, mapping out points of growth, and deciding on definite objectives to which the entire digital transformation would make much difference or contribute significantly. A properly developed vision must be effectively disseminated to all stakeholders- partners, customers, and employees-if consensus and buy-in are ever to be elicited. The clear vision provides direction and inspiration to the business through its complicated journey of digital transformation.

The devices of the digital transformation projects will be the main devices of new technology adoption. Every business has to consider and decide on the best technology that suits their operational needs, as well as their strategic goals. This shall be done through the implementation of cloud computing, big data analytics, artificial intelligence, and the Internet of Things, among others. This would mean that all these technologies have certain advantages and powers, which could be facilitators of change in themselves. While cloud computing brings flexibility and scalability, AI expands decision-making and accelerates processes. Appropriate technology selection comes after an assessment of plausible impacts and integrations that are in tune with the long-term vision of the organization. Equally important is the reengineering process for corporations to leverage digital technologies. Most often, new technical capabilities render traditional ways of doing things obsolete and inefficient. Tactical strategy in digital transformation should bring specific emphasis on detailed analysis regarding the existence of processes in terms of redundancies, inefficiencies, and spaces that offer room for improvement. Process reengineering refers to the reimagining of workflows in order to apply and utilize fully digital tools and technologies. This would involve automating activities that are considered drudgery, smoothing and streamlining processes, new digital ideas, and other ways of doing business that will enhance productivity and customers. Process reengineering helps organizations improve productivity, reduce costs, and generally perform well.

One very important but usually overlooked area of digital transformation is that of cultural change. Successful digital transformation, therefore, requires changes in corporate culture to adapt to digital ways of working and thinking. Cultural shift involves fostering an attitude that emphasizes creativity, adaptability, and continuous improvement. To make this work, leaders have to drive this change through modeling digital behaviors, experimenting, fostering a growth mindset, support, and engaging workers in the process. Give them tools and training that would help them not only cope with the new ways of working but also new technologies. In other words, a cultural approach towards digital transformation is absolutely key to overcoming the resistance and making it successful on a sustainable basis. The second most important element in the design of digital transformation is the aspect of customer experience. In the digital world, the expectations have flipped, and it is a bare necessity to change with those needs. Digital transformation enables better customer relationships: multichannel engagement in real-time with personalized experiences. Such technologies include digital marketing platforms, data analytics, and CRM, through which an organization may have insight into its customers' needs, interests, and behaviors. In return, this would have the businesses serve them with personalized experiences and, thereby, ensure higher satisfaction, loyalty, and advocacy.

Analytics and data management form the major share of all digital transformation plans. If the collection, analysis, and utilization of data are done correctly, it provides enormous insight that aids decision-making. More importantly, this encompasses the development of a proper data strategy pertaining to analytics competency, data quality, and governance. Most importantly, there is a dire need for data management technologies to be developed with the necessary platforms and mechanisms so that the collection, storage, and analysis of data are done effortlessly. Additionally, with advanced analytics techniques, such as prescriptive and predictive analytics, businesses are able to find patterns and interpret opportunities to make improved decisions. A well-articulated data strategy unlocks a pathway to innovation enabled or key strategic objectives realized through the exploitation of data. Change management forms an important constituent element of any strategy related to digital transformation. New methods for the implementation of processes and technology will make quite an impact on the current workflows and require considerable adjustment. Effective change management is sensitive to employee concerns and responds to the need for adjustment through training and resource tools. The design of a formal change management plan that outlines the training curricula, communication tactics, and support systems forms part of the approaches involved in the planning and supporting of the change. It can only be done with early employee involvement in smoothing the transition and effective adoption of new technologies, overcoming employee resistance, and constantly offering support.

The leadership has to drive and sustain digital transformation: leaders should primarily allocate resources, define clear objectives, and support initiatives for transformation. Besides, they will develop a novel and collaborative culture so that all staff will receive the digital advances and participate in the process of transformation. Through the development of vision and strategy, good leadership engages people at all levels by resolving problems and issues and celebrating quick wins. The dedicated leader of digital transformation inspires his team to take the business toward its goals of transformation. Besides monitoring internal factors, an organization should keep a continuous scan of the external environment for forces that might influence its effort toward digital transformation. It would also cover market trends, legal specifications, and competitive dynamics. The organization can only pre-estimate the change, find alternatives to its strategies, and locate new opportunities by being knowledgeable concerning external influences. Interacting with the right professionals in various industry events and undertaking market research will yield good insight into the external factors of digital transformation. In this regard, organizations can hence develop strategies that take into consideration these external factors relevant to the larger business environment and in tandem with industry best practices.

Finally, results from digital transformation initiatives should be monitored and measured for continuous improvement. Well-set metrics and KPIs will be pivotal in making the organization measure the impact of its digital transformation on different aspects of the businesses. It involves the measurement of newly developed technology and redesigned procedures effectiveness, clients' satisfaction, and staff's satisfaction. It also consists of the identification of areas that need improvement, the right adjustment in strategies, and seeing that expected results were achieved through transformation activities. This could be possible through continuous analysis of these indicators and KPIs every now and then. This will, in turn, be supported by the constant improvement of the ways to measure digital transformation in support of the succeeding steps toward continued success and the accomplishment of goals in the future. In brief, only with the implementation of strategies for digital transformation will enterprises be able to pass through the challenge of the digital era with pride and achieve their strategic goals. This will develop a proper vision, appropriate technologies, reengineering processes, drive cultural change, improve customer experience, manage data, and put in place appropriate change management techniques that will successfully drive transformation in organizations. If the process of digital transformation is to be affected, what is mostly required is leadership, outside variables, and continuous assessment, which will make the process effective and sustainable. Since it is a conscious approach to influence deep change, with the help of digital technologies, an organization will achieve high-scale performance, competitiveness, and overall success.

Data-Driven Decision Making

Data-driven decision making has emerged as a prime differentiator in modern corporate strategy, wherein firms can arrive at decisions on the basis of actual facts and evidence rather than on a guess or gut feeling. Indeed, data are everywhere, and technology keeps evolving with breathtaking rapidity. The usage of data within decisions helps organizations enhance their productivity and competitiveness; it nurtures innovation. With all the potentials applied, each business would be able to enhance its processes, consumer behaviors, and market trends. To that respect, they may make such decisions that would turn out wiser and more successful in the future. Data-driven decision-making may, in principle, be carried out through systematic collection, analysis, and interpretation of data to inform business decisions. That is in contrast to traditional methods, where decisions are made based on anecdotal information and subjective judgments. Data-driven decision making-your very basic idea behind the importance of statistical analytics and quantitative data-basically alters how decisions are made. Data-driven decisions derive their power from objective insights into the data that helps make the decisions. This may reduce biases and make results more accurate.

Of course, the very first most important thing in adopting data-driven decision-making is to build a concrete infrastructure for storing and managing data. That means designing efficient processes and mechanisms for capturing, storing, and managing the data. In this respect, it requires investment in a range of data management technologies and platforms that are capable of aggregating information emanating from sources such as internal systems, external market research, and consumer interactions. There is also a concern over data quality, as one needs timely, complete, and accurate data to determine trustworthy insights. Because of this, data governance structures should be put in place that stipulate how the data is to be managed and used concerning the sustenance of data security and integrity. Unless effective data architecture is set up, a section or organization cannot get into the analytics layer. In such data, much information for trends, patterns, and insight extraction can be availed using statistical techniques and analytical tools. This can further be supported by incorporating advanced analytics such as machine learning and artificial intelligence capable of showing complex relationships and enabling forecast future occurrences. The insights will make more sense to the decision-maker only when provided in an easily accessible and understandable format; hence, decision-makers will have to be supported with data visualization tools. Only beyond the analytical stage, when an organization has very strong analytical capabilities, translation of insights into decisions will show opportunities for improvement and better insight into business surroundings.

It is between the evaluation and the actionability of the data insights that decision-makers stand to match the analytical outcomes to operational needs and strategic goals. In this respect, a culture valuing insight from data- or briefly, a data-driven insight-will in turn nurture employees' literacy on such competencies. The degree of analysis and interpretation of data-driven insights among employees can be enhanced through training and development programs. It could be a gradual change in corporate outlook to become more data-driven in perspective. More importantly, the framing of the decision-making process should be done in a way that data-driven insights could form part of the basis for making decisions, ensuring recommendations driven by data are presented before decisions are taken, considering other factors such as market conditions, legal requirements, and business objectives. Data-driven decisions allow business views to be realistic and comprehensive for most aspects that may enhance organizational performance. From analyzed customer behavior and preference, data-driven marketing strategies may point toward ways to ensure increased success of campaigns. Such data-driven insights may further allow businesses to segment their customer base, hence creating targeted campaigns at specific groups with personalized messages to improve customer engagement and conversion rates. It will be useful during operations to make insight-driven decisions through the analysis of the level of inventory, the trend of demand, and performance of suppliers to attain maximum efficiency in the supply chain. It will be cost-effective and enhance service expectations by putting the company in a good position where they will be making well-versed decisions on procurements, logistics, and inventories.

Arguably, the most important benefits that accrue through techniques of data-driven decision-making relate to improvements in strategic planning and forecasting. Given that it conducts an analysis based on trends and patterns that have already occurred in the past, future performance and market conditions can be gauged quite rightly. For that predictive potential, businesses could prepare for changes in advance, adapt to them proactively, and avoid as much risk as possible. For instance, data-driven forecasting could allow business financial planning whereby the firms get financial forecasts of revenues and expenses, evaluate any likely financial issues, and then strategize contingency approaches. It might also result in a high success rate of the launched product as decisions on very critical features of the product, its price, and positioning in the market could be detected from the early stages of product development. However, while there is a list of several advantages provided by data-driven decision-making, there are a few disadvantages, too, which a business should be fully aware of. Among the key issues are security and privacy concerns related to the data. An organization must be sure that in collecting and processing big data it keeps within the bounds of the law on data protection and retains sensitive information. Besides, it is justified on the part of an organization to adopt necessary security measures concerning encryption and access controls so that information gets protected against data breaches and unauthorized access. Further, consent by the owners of such information is required, and its use on the part of the organization should be with utter transparency.

The second challenge could be the smothering due to volumes of data. The volume of data for an organization may raise challenges in underlining most relevant and valuable insights. They should, instead focus on developing appropriate strategies of data and filter out key indicators based on priorities. Data aggregation and filtering strategies could, therefore, be implemented; this would allow the management of the complexity regarding data and ensure that the decision-makers would always get access to the most relevant information. The process of data-driven decision-making also involves overcoming the aversion to change and creating an attitude toward it. Employees may be more used to traditional modes of decision-making processes and may be skeptical when heavy reliance is placed on data. Various case studies regarding success in data-driven decision making could be employed by the organizations to show its advantage in problem solving. Because leadership sets the pace to show how data is to be used and valued in the organization, leadership support is very important in effecting this cultural change.

Data-driven decision-making thus easily slips into habitual routine within an organizational culture of experimentation, continuous learning, and curiosity. Data-driven decision making is a powerful approach to increase organizational performance and achieve strategic objectives. Therefore, this would mean superior quality, accuracy, and speed in decision-making from data architecture up to the advanced usage of analytics and infusion of insight. Some of the key rewards of data-driven decision-making include the following: from operations to marketing to financial planning up to product creation. But each step of the way, in making this journey to unlock value from data-driven decision-making, an organization must cross a host of hurdles involving issues pertaining to data privacy, data overload, and cultural resistance. That is, it will be because of data quality, analytical capabilities, and culture that are supportive enough for an organization to press forward and ring success to stay competitive in the digital era.

Enhancing Customer Experience through Technology

It was thus that the technology-enhanced customer experience became the critical strategy that finally met and overcame the permanent changes that took place in the expectations of their clients. This has thus enabled businesses today to implement digital tools and platforms in designing seamless experiences, at the same time personalizing experiences to the engagement of more possibilities than ever. It is the integration of technology into customer experience initiatives that sets firms up for success in the market by making customers happier and more loyal all at once. So, how can technology be applied to improve customer experiences? I will focus on automation, data analytics, omnichannel engagement, personalization, and emerging technologies. It has been built that technology in the areas of personalization improving experiences, for example, tended to develop into a few cardinal ways. The use of information and technology creates experiences in front of the customer by appealing to the tastes and behaviors of the world, commanding companies to apply the practice of personal interaction. This can be achieved by the use of AI and machine learning; whereby business companies process the huge volume of data generated by customers in order to find trends and preferences. Actually, this is the reason business conducts a study to make offers, recommendations, and messages tailored to each one of their personal customers' needs. Because of this, it would also be more like any e-commerce website where recommendation algorithms would suggest products to the customers depending on their history of browsing and past purchases. Such personalization engagements not only heighten customer delight but also promise loyalty and better conversion rates.

The second most important feature of the use of technology in enhancing customer experience is omnichannel interaction. Today's consumers engage brands on so many touchpoints, from social media and websites to mobile apps and brick-and-mortar. Integrated correctly, it can be the key enabler for an organization to provide frictionless, consistently seamless experiences for a customer. Technology will create the key to a unified consumer profile, cross-channel interaction, and real-time updating. CRM systems and omnichannel platforms maintain relevance and consistency in the interaction with them, proof that they keep the data of the customer in sync with touchpoints. A very good example could be when a customer has been interacting with a brand on social media; he feels the same when he visits the website or any mobile application of the company. This would allow companies to exploit this competency and extend their relationships to everything that improves consumer satisfaction, hence providing easy delivery across touchpoints. Other company technologies that can support organizations in improving customer experience are the automation of perfect communication and productivity. The presented automation solutions, including chatbots and email automation, create opportunities for companies to make sure services are timely and proper, hence freeing human labor from agents. The AI-driven chatbot, for example, is able to answer frequent customers' questions, process transactions, reset passwords, and help consumers with other generic queries on the spot. In this way, the consumer is being serviced after work hours, and he is saving time to get a response. Automation promotes efficiency in internal processes; hence, support staff engaged in customer support focuses on higher-value and more complex interactions. All this makes automation enable companies to move faster, more efficiently, and more consistently, hence the enhancement of customer experience.

Data analytics is important in enhancing customer experience, as it provides insightful information concerning the needs, tastes, and behaviors of customers. The data can be sourced from social media, surveys, and customer interactions using advanced analytics technologies when assessed. This analytics-driven approach enables the enterprise to trace the trend and hence make more informed decisions with regard to understanding the customer. For instance, one is capable of analyzing sentiments and feedback from clients to single out areas of concern and, out of it, proactively work on mitigating the problems before they start blowing out of proportion. This will also place the organization in a good position of being able to predict future behaviors and preferences of its customers, which are important in estimating demand and offering personalized experiences. Data analytics enables organizations to improve consumer satisfaction and make wiser decisions in furtherance of their services. The second most influential driver into the future of consumer experience involves emerging technology. Also, VR and AR are emergent technologies, just like the concept of the Internet of Things, that exist to deal with customers in new ways and implant them into experiences. Both virtual and augmented reality will be a personal environment because of the individual communication and presentation of information, experiences, and multi-product demonstrations. For example, any furniture store can give buyers an idea of what some piece of furniture might look like in your house before they buy it using augmented reality. Down the line of similar ideas and thoughts, IoT devices have the capability to drive customer experiences with real-time data and customized interactions. In fact, smart home appliances can go about repetitive chores in an even more automated fashion for each customer's preference, making recommendations based on the same. Emergent technologies can be creatively used to develop new innovative customer experiences in ways that differentiate the company from the competition.

There are many areas of potential that technology has to improve the experience of the consumer, but businesses first have to become vigilant against the pitfalls and make sure the application of technology is done in a manner that suits it. The most basic issue relates to the amount of automation deployed against human touch. While this does bring a great amount of efficiency through automation, it is equally important that lines of live support stay open at any given moment, should this become necessary. Frictionless experiences involve automated and human interactions that businesses use to attend to and manage situations that are complex-needing humans. The question begs itself now: how are the security and privacy of the data ensured? Where the businesses involved in the collection and processing of sensitive information the consumers have to be liable for the protection of such information. Besides, a great security system has to create confidence via the protection of data from the customer. This includes encryption as well as access controls. The organizations need to form laws concerning the enforcement regime with regard to data protection; agencies need to be very transparent regarding the collecting, usage, and storing of customers' data. Where the data is given a reason for privacy and security by firms, then customers will trust their brands and enhance the overall experience.

To keep competitive and achieve such evolving expectations, driven customers themselves-deployment of technology has become a must for any firm. Indeed, automation, data analytics, personalization, omnichannel engagement, and the use of emergent technologies place an organization at the bleeding edge of innovation in friction-free, engaging experiences that drive consumer satisfaction and loyalty. Whatever that might be, companies have to remember imperatives like the safety and privacy of data as they walk this tightrope balance between automation and the human touch. What that means is that at the end of the day, while companies have to take strategic approaches towards technology, in front of all that technology comes customer needs. This would leave them with satisfied customers, improve relations with them, and be successful in the long run.

Future-Proofing Your Business

The pace of technological change, the vagaries of consumer whims, and the variable fortunes of economics-all have become simple constants to any business participating in today's turbulent sector. It is regarding these factors that consideration about future-proofing needs to be brought into discussion. Leading through change, embracing emergent trends, creating a base for longevity: these stand as ways an organization can remain resilient, competitive. In other words, the future-proofing should be holistic: from risk management to organizational agility, technology investment, and strategic planning; it will enable the businesses to thrive despite many uncertainties. The first thought in the future-proofing of an enterprise would relate to a forward-looking strategy that would lead towards market trends and be congenial with long-term objectives. Deep market research and analysis are the basic pre-requisites for understanding new trends, client needs, and competitive dynamics. Firms have to upgrade their strategic plans from time to time so that they remain updated and relevant in the world of changing scenarios. The identification of potential opportunities and threats that the companies avail themselves of realigns their strategies to achieve or sustain market competitiveness. A clear strategic vision provides a focal point for the firms and instills them with the confidence to handle uncertainty.

Investment in Technology: Investments in technology are the keys towards the future-proofing of any company. As long as warp-speed technological advances continue, scaling up businesses that intend to sustain competitive advantage will have to go on. Resources are likely to be reviewed and consolidated towards such technologies that enhance efficiency in operations and customer satisfaction for business growth. An example could be cloud computing, AI, data analytics, and automation tools. Securing such technologies into innovative solutions helps organizations gain insight, caters to the dynamic needs of the market, and streamlines processes. Companies that invest in technology are best positioned to exploit emerging opportunities and stay relevant. The other critical component in future-proofing the corporation is organizational agility. Most fundamentally, the capability of being agile-to respond to the changing circumstance in time and seize new opportunities-makes all the difference between long-term success and failure. That means every business has to develop a really innovative and adaptive culture in which the employees can accept and enjoy constant change and continuous improvement. It's a matter of designing flexible structures and processes that enable fast decision-making and responsiveness. For project and product development management, agile practices such as Scrum or Kanban have been adapted for superior performance. Agility can enable companies to respond to shifts in the marketplace, advances in technology, and customer requests, making the business resilient and competitive.

Risk management is about future-proofing your company. It allows an organization to reduce adverse events but also to prepare better for uncertainties through the identification and reduction of potential risks. This involves threat assessment-both external and internal-developing contingency plans, and strategies that mitigate risks. The list includes managing supply chain disruption, cybersecurity breaches, change in legislation, and economic decline. Through active risk management, a firm can continue with operations and protection of capital; hence, its activities would be sustainable even under challenges. Regular risk auditing and scenario planning enable companies to predict certain problems that may happen and help them come up with viable solutions. Future-proofing your organization has something to do with customer-centricity. Understanding and catering to the needs and whims of customers will, in turn, secure long-term relationships that will drive growth. It is an opportunity that businesses should seize through strategic investments in methodologies and research, added to customers' feedback, with a view to realizing their expectations and pain issues. That means data analytics must be applied to find out the trends and patterns that guide marketing plans, customer support, and product development. It can only be actualized in terms of customer expectation and loyalty with more personalization and bespoke experiences. Indeed, businesses that prioritize customer experience, taking action upon the shift in preference, prove that customer satisfaction will soar high, repeat businesses will take place, and strong brand reputation will come about.

The key lever to future-proof a firm is innovation. Innovation culture allows businesses to explore ideas, come up with creative solutions, and beat their competition. They have to inspire experimentation, invest in research and development in order to beat their business regarding market trends. They must create the enabling environment where staff can share ideas on creative ideas and collaborate on projects. This may go all the way to alliances and collaborations with startups, academia, and technology companies in regard to access to new technologies and knowledge. Businesses are to innovate and keep a lead during turbulence in the markets.

It is time for businesses to future-proof their firms through sustainability. With increased awareness environmentally and socially, the onus in business is to prove themselves ethical enough in answering questions to do with sustainability. This is the time for environmental processes: waste management, energy efficiency, and sourcing of commodities whose production is responsive to sustainability. Other activities include social responsibility involving community support, diversity, and inclusion. If sustainability is among the core values and core operations of the businesses, they will be able to attract the socially conscious consumers, improve their brand reputation, and at the same time follow recent legislation. Talent management and employee development are part of the major focus areas in order for a business to be future-proof. After all, knowledgeable and motivated teams are needed in the attainment of strategic goals, innovation, and the adoption of changes. For that, employee training and development is particularly important in businesses to enhance the capability or capacity of a firm. Training can be on-the-job education, career enhancement, or professional growth.

The organization should give support in terms of work environment, too, regarding attracting and retaining talents within the company. Organizations definitely have to focus much more on people development and welfare outcomes, as these definitely have a direct effect on the level of performance and productivity.

The key to making an organization future-proof lies in integrating technology into daily operations within the overall strategic planning process. Admittedly, new technologies would keep on emerging, but from those very exciting ones which may help bring improvement quite radically into many diverse elements of corporate operation, examples are augmented reality and blockchain. The examples include augmented reality for immersive consumer experiences, blockchain for a secure supply chain. In doing so, an executive needs to continuously update himself on the emergence of new technologies and assess their potential use in applications. That is how strategic anticipation of what technology can bring into the future allows companies to be aware of what kind of emerging technologies and what advantages they would like to use with it, in order for them to keep pace ahead of the curve.

The multimodal approach basically rests in the risk management abilities of organizations, strategic planning, investments in technologies, and customers focused on future-proofing one's company. Other important things include developing a future-focused strategy, investing in technology, driving agility, managing risk, and driving customer experience towards new levels-all these help businesses move with change and be flexible in the marketplace. Emphasized commitment to innovative and sustainable development, along with that of people, creates formidable foundations that will make sure success is guaranteed long into the future.

CHAPTER IV

Developing an Innovation Roadmap

Setting Innovation Goals and Objectives

Setting innovation goals and objectives is highly instrumental for companies in the quest for growth, competitiveness, and survival in a dynamic business environment. However, innovation, on its part, can never be pursued for its sake but rather as a means towards new value creation, satisfaction of consumer needs, and gaining competitive advantage. Organizations should set well-defined and realistic goals in line with their strategic vision regarding the successful exploitation of innovation. This section discusses why innovation goals should be set, highlights key considerations supposed to factor in such goal development, and addresses the implementation required for such goals and measures that mean success.

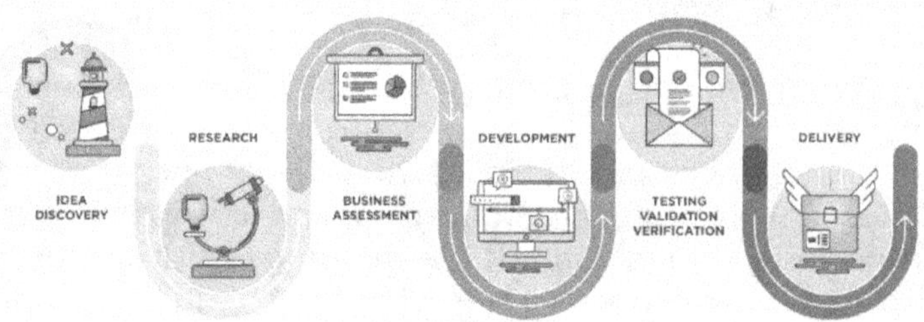

Of these, the first is that clear innovation goals and objectives are required in the light of a strategic vision for the organization. Innovations have to be aligned with overall corporate strategy if they are to support big objectives and bring value. Organizations must identify their long-term goals to be achieved and analyze how innovation can enable them to be realized. It would require keeping a constant eye on consumer needs, changes in market conditions, and competitor dynamics as a basis for timely, appropriate decisions regarding where innovation is likely to generate the greatest return. Following the example above, if an organization's strategic objective is market share, its innovation activity is targeted at developing products or services that meet the unmet needs of its target markets. In coordinating the goals of innovation with strategic vision, one can ensure the activities concerned with innovation become relevant and meaningful. Whereby at the setting of this strategic backdrop, organizations are then able to set certain targeted and quantified goals and objectives of innovation. Setting specific, clearly defined goals will enable the firm to stay on target and achieve its innovative goals. Objectives must be exact and measurable for one to monitor progress in case one wants to evaluate progress. Examples include "Develop and launch three new products within the next 18 months". In this case, examples of certain objectives will consist of: "Complete market research by the end of Q1" and "Finalize product prototypes by the end of Q3". Well-set and quantifiable objectives realize a systematic approach to achieving innovation in organizations whereby activities are channeled to realize such objectives.

The second key thing that should be considered is ensuring that the objectives of innovation are ambitious yet achievable. While such objectives should urge a company to strive for excellence and explore untried ways, objectives of innovation should also be realistic and attainable. Where modest ambition will not attain meaningful development, over-ambitious goals stir frustration and disengagement. Organizations need to take a great look in the mirror at their resources, competencies, and constraints and pursue an appropriate level. This includes reflections about the culture of the company, the talent, the technology, and the money. Setting stretching but realistic ambitions will enable organizations to inspire their people while keeping a realistic focus on what is achievable. Setting successful innovation goals and objectives involves collaboration and cross-functional cooperation; many times, innovation is based on input from and supported by a number of organizational divisions and a number of stakeholders. This is because the setting of goals with different perspectives and opinions is facilitated by the input of teams that may emanate from other sections such as operations, marketing, and research and development. The fact that a collective setting of goals takes place also facilitates common understanding and integration within the enterprise innovation projects. The ownership of the project by team members and commitment to the same culminates in the realization of results.

While setting targets related to innovation, companies need to consider not only internal collaboration but also those forces from the outside that influence them. Innovation priorities have a great influence in general on competitive dynamics, market developments, and customer feedback. It is relevant for organizations to keep themselves updated with industry advancement and to take into account third-party input in the target formulation process. It would contain market data, consideration regarding the needs of clients, and monitoring activity of competition in order to outline opportunities and risks. Considering these types of external factors, the organizations set their innovation targets sensitive to the demands of the market and can locate them effectively within the competitive arena. The setting of innovation goals and objectives should result in a commitment of resources with an action plan. This means that there is a formulation of an action plan which states the tasks required to attain each objective with stated responsibility and time limitations. It would contain major deliverables and milestones, containing how the progress is to be monitored and any impediment to progress overcome. Resource mobilization would also be appropriate since some innovation projects do indeed call for investments in infrastructure, human resources, and technology. It is in the strategic allocation of resources that organizations can find a way to innovate and make sure all teams are bonded with resources and support for success.

Setting and achieving goals of innovation should be made by constant monitoring and assessment of the progress. Organizations should, therefore, institute metrics and KPIs to measure innovation projects' performance and test the achievements of goals set. It enables periodic assessment and review that correctly identifies areas of achievement and further development. The success of innovation ventures is indicated through different quantitative measures, including the number of releases of new products, revenue generated through innovations, and levels of customer satisfaction. Firms can also continuously monitor and assess the result of the process of innovation, make decisions based on evidence, and reconsider their strategy if and where necessary in light of whether or not goals on innovation are achieved. Setting goals and working towards the realization of goals pertaining to innovation has to be done with a level of flexibility and adaptation. Companies work in dynamic environments, and it is only possible to achieve some of the set goals because some obstacles or changes cannot be predicted. It should, hence, always be on the lookout so that it can change objectives or goals, either because more information becomes available or the market change presents new opportunities. Therefore, the culture needs to be open and flexible, with teams empowered to look again at goals and make adjustments wherever necessary. With this, organizations can thrive in this position of uncertainty for flexibility and unleash innovation.

Communication at every level of innovation goals and progress keeps engagement and alignment alive. The more transparent the communication, the better all the members of the team are in regard to goals being pursued, what their roles in those achievements are, and how things are going. Regular updates, feedback meetings, and pursued accomplishments create a work climate that is upbeat and motivational. In addition to the pursuit of innovations, effective communication provides insight into the necessity for the attainment of set goals. It helps an enterprise to develop a corporate culture that is co-operative and goal-oriented since the stakeholders are made informed and involved in this process. Setting goals and objectives concerning innovation becomes of utmost importance for growth and sustenance of competitive advantage in today's fast-moving corporate world. Innovation objectives can become more systematic and deliberate by establishing the innovation objectives with respect to strategic vision, their further processing in operating goal format, and making goals challenging yet attainable. Implementation involves the ability to resource effectively, involve externals to bring in ideas and collaborate. Finally, retain the flexibility for the desired outcome. It simply means that businesses go a long way in coping with uncertainty and new opportunities if the culture of adaptation and frankness in communication is encouraged. Where innovation objectives are set up and realized in a conscious and systematic way, businesses will be better equipped to innovate, adapt to markets in a timely manner, and encourage success that is long-term.

Designing an Innovation Framework

A framework for innovations should be designed for organizations that want to promote creativity systematically for technological improvements in order to retain market competitiveness, which changes day by day. Efficient innovation frameworks are capable of making a structured process that enables the finding, creating, and implementation of new ideas that support the achievement of the strategic objectives of an organization. It, therefore, concerns processes, tools, and organizational structures that not only allow for innovation to take place but also ensure its integration into the core business process. This section discusses some key elements and considerations that one must have at the back of his mind when an innovation framework is under development and also emphasizes the role of the framework in attaining innovative success and long-term growth. First, any strategy of innovation needs to define a very clear vision and strategic goals. The framework for innovation must be in line with the firm's long-term objectives and overall strategy. Stated goals and objectives for the innovation effort define what innovation means to the company. For instance, the organization may want to innovate in customer experience, operational efficiency, or the creation of a product. From there, it could enable organizations to drive focused and meaningful innovation through the articulation of an innovation vision in concert with strategic priorities, allowing them to focus on the initiatives that have the greatest potential value.

The second important component of this framework for innovation is a well-defined process for generating and evaluating ideas. This would be supportive in organizing the collection, assessment, and selection of ideas of creative value. They come via innovation contests, suggestion platforms, or brainstorming. These ideas thus require a systemic check in terms of their feasibility, potential impact, and strategic alignment. Other criteria that form part of such an evaluation process are commercial potential, technical feasibility, and financial viability. Companies can ensure highly valued ideas are found and pursued to successful completion by establishing structured processes for the generation and assessment of the concept. Building innovation on the company's culture or creating an innovative culture is a part of creating an innovation framework. It is important that there be a supporting culture to allow experimentation, teamwork, and creativity. It is at this junction that organizing should create an enabling culture in which employees are free to share ideas and take risks. In other words, there must be avenues through which ideas can be shared freely, recognized, and, where possible, rewards given for such innovative ideas; tools which would encourage experimentation. Innovation culture requires leadership as an example, facilitation in innovating, and provision of necessary resources. It will help an organization to create a culture that inspires innovation, creativity, and continuous improvement by integrating innovative culture.

An innovative framework can only be successfully implemented with effective resource allocation. In other ways, innovation basically translates to investment in many ways: finance, talent, and technology. Organizations need to take appropriate action in the light of resource allocation so that innovation activities are able to equip the right kind of tools and competencies for success. This would include investment in R&D, training, and development of the staff members, along with the acquisition of newer technologies. The companies must also allow for the making of budget provision for the innovation initiatives taken up and ensure the resources are used efficiently towards a better return on investment. It is with efficient resource allocation that companies can develop their innovative capabilities further in the attainment of planned outcomes. A good innovation structure should have mechanisms for scaling up and monitoring innovation. Organizations need mechanisms that track the development of new ideas from conception into implementation and integrate these into existing practice. This shall be done by developing project management plans, defining the responsibilities and roles, dates of milestones, and completion.

The organization should develop strategies for partnerships, market entry, and commercialization apart from scaling the ideas that prove successful. Scaling requires much frontloading of preparation and coordination to ensure that the introduction and adoption of innovations are effective. Setting mechanisms for managing and scaling innovation inward will definitely enhance the organization's capability to introduce new ideas to the market for growth. Evaluation and feedback are part of an innovation framework. To this effect, organizations should avail mechanisms of monitoring progress and reviewing the outcomes so that innovation efforts result in something fruitful and in line with the organizational objectives. This would involve a number of activities that include setting up key performance indicators, taking contributions from stakeholders involved, and carrying out regular reviews that track the success of projects in innovation. While evaluation and feedback bring into focus areas where there is scope for improvement, simultaneously they give valuable data on how the innovation framework works. This is information that an organization should capitalize on in terms of improving processes, revising strategies, and reducing concerns that might emerge. It is through continuous assessment and analysis that an organization refines its setup to achieve success in the long term.

Partnerships and collaborative relationships are the other necessary components of a healthy innovation framework. Innovating with external partners-start-ups, academic institutes, and technology vendors-are no longer novel or unexpected. As a matter of fact, with collaboration comes the ability to have access to new markets, skills, and technology. They have got to look for alliances that would further their cause and strengthen the reason for innovation. The license agreement, joint ventures, and strategic partnerships are examples of this. Through various external collaborations, an organization gets a competitive advantage in terms of new insights and a faster pace of innovation. Only transparency and communication are the ways through which an innovation framework gets well implemented. Open and frank communications help in making all the parties well informed about objectives, procedures, and development regarding innovation. It would also involve updating the staff and other stakeholders with the goals and vision of the framework of innovation, showing details about the projects underway besides seeking their input. Most importantly, transparency will encourage involvement and foster trust by devising a common understanding of the innovative initiative. Due to increased collaboration and alignment of effort through effective communication and transparency in place, organizations will be able to lock in successful innovation outcomes.

The ability for change and readjustment of the framework of innovation according to the change in trend and circumstance would ensure success in the long run. Organizations must adopt agile and sensitive practices constantly towards new changes that are happening within the dynamic business environment. For this, the framework of innovation needs periodic review and updating so that changes in priorities of the organization, market fluctuation, and technological advancement are accounted for. This requires initiative on the part of the enterprise to identify new trends and opportunities. Update the innovation framework, and the organization starts staying ahead of the curve and drives innovation effectively. It involves prudent development of culture, objectives setting, process formalization, and resource distribution in developing an innovation framework. Other components that are indispensable in innovation frameworks include the generation and evaluation of ideas, cultural support, resource management and scaling, assessment and feedback, cooperation, communication, and flexibility. An integrated, structured approach to innovation will drive the process of innovation in a systematic manner, continuously adapt to evolving conditions, and realize long-term success within organizations. The effective innovation framework trains success toward long-term existence along with enhancing the ability of the organization in creating and executing the newness in the fiercely competitive, changing industry.

Funding Innovation Initiatives

Funding innovation projects has something to do with inspiring creativity, creating new technology, and driving organizational growth. Most innovations require huge investments in research and development, as well as in the implementation and scaling up of new ideas. Strategies that ensure funding will be effective in enabling innovation projects to have all that is required for success to provide value. The section will attempt to explore some of the innovative aspects of project financing-identification of sources of funds, management of finance, and calculation of returns on investment. Identification and securing adequate sources of finance is the first step in financing the innovation efforts. Innovation in a business entity may be funded by various techniques that include hybrid techniques, external money, and internal. The use of funding from the corporation's budget is what characterizes internal finance. This may be more than appropriation of a budget that is derived from budgetary cuts from less important fields or even from the event of a creative project having its own self-contained budget. Ready availability and consistency with the goals of the organization outlined within the strategies are the chief advantages of internal finance. It may, however, be bounded by present financial constraints and even lobbying within its ranks.

Apart from the budget and finance at its disposal, the supply within the organization is augmented by external money, which emanates from various possible sources. Other sources of such investments common for new and fast-expanding companies are venture capital along private equity. These investors usually invest in those companies in return for stock stakes, apart from providing extra support through industry networks and strategic advice. Other sources of external finance are government grants and subsidies, normally offered in return for research and development promotion in a particular field or sector of the economy. This is sometimes competitive and the funding may have attached criteria to be met by organizations on top of showing that the project they want to carry out will be beneficial. Other external options include investors' angels, crowdsourcing, and collaborations of businesses. Organizations may consider these in light of their specific needs and objectives since each has its respective advantages and disadvantages. After identifying sources of funds for funding innovation efforts, management would then need to put these resources into effective and efficient use. This is further realized through budgeting: financial planning and management are important in driving innovation initiatives through budgeting-that is, cost estimates, funding, and monitoring of expenditure. The budgetary plan should be highly detailed, showing at each step in the innovation chain the financial requirements from initial research and development to commercialization. This would involve cost estimates relating to labor, supplies, and technology, among other things. Proper apportionment of funds avoids over-investment and scarcity of funds, besides ensuring that the worthiest activities are supported in sufficient measure.

Cost monitoring and control represent integral features of any good budgetary management in the innovation process. Regular analysis of financial records and expenditures against the budget, therefore, provides scope for the organizations to identify any variance and initiate immediate remedial measures. The cost control strategies will thus be useful in managing projects by negotiating with suppliers, making use of resources in the most feasible capacity, and bringing outgoing expenses to a close. The formulation of financial metrics along with the measurement of performance will enable benchmarking the progress of innovation initiatives with respect to economic viability. If an organization can keep a healthy system of budgetary control, then it is all set to achieve any objectives that it may have in regard to innovation while at the same time assuring maximization of return value for any investment. Talent One of the biggest considerations with investing in innovation efforts will be determining the return on investment or, better still ROI. By definition, the return on investment is the net financial benefit of an innovation project against the cost of investment involved. An analysis of return on investment, therefore, enables the organization to understand the effectiveness of funding and make informed decisions about future investments. Different ways through which return on investment could be ascertained by making an analysis of innovation effects include cost-saving, increment of market shares, and revenue growth. Other gains to organizations that are non-monetary include enhanced competitive advantages, reputations of brands, as well as satisfaction from customers. This will allow the organizations to critically measure the general performance of their operations in innovations and fully comprehend the impact as a result of financial and monetary gains assessment.

On the other hand, organizational innovations should be checked for strategic fit and whether or not they may serve for a long period of time more than financial metrics. Strategic alignment deals with the extent to which the innovation initiative supports or furthers the general aims and objectives of the company. This will imply that projects supportive of the strategic priorities of an organization are likely to yield successful long-term results with substantial value delivery. Long-term potential impact, in this respect, concerns a review of sustainability, scalability, and market potential. To this end, an innovation answering the emerging customer wants and addressing the emerging trends and wide diffusion potential is likely to pay off over time. The second important element in the financing of projects on innovation is that of risk management. Indeed, the very nature of innovation risk and uncertainty recommends preparedness on the part of companies for any obstacle in the course of work. Organizations would identify and evaluate those risks that are likely to be faced-like technological failure, market acceptance problems, and budgetary constraints devise ways would mitigate these. Insurance, scenario analysis, and contingency planning are a few methods through which organizations may try to manage uncertainty and secure their investment when running businesses. The organization should not be flexible about strategy and hence can easily change its method of fundraising if the circumstances alter.

Partnership brings in more funding as a result of innovative projects. For example, partners bring with them money, knowledge, and assistance. The likelihood of working in partnership with outsiders will be a grant of access to innovative technologies, specialized knowledge, and complementary resources. Examples of such partners include institutions of research, technology providers, and industry groups. Partnerships spread out the individual risks and may share the financial burden for innovation ventures. Joint-venture and strategic partnership may have access to capital, markets, and resources. It would be expected that a trusting relationship would be set up with the stakeholders and partners, too, which could lead to joint gain, co-investment, and shared learning. Innovation funding is best managed through open communication and building trust. It would involve status, challenges, and results coming out of projects to which the stakeholders would show continued support and confidence. Transparency in communication would imply that data with regard to project milestones, overall impact, and financial performance are shared. The participative environment justifies the process of innovation at stakeholder levels-be it consumer, employee, or investor. This will mean that all financing decisions will be duly informed and supported, unraveling of problems can be duly endorsed, and expectations managed. In innovating a project, one will also require a financing plan that considers thorough budgeting, acquisition of resources, and return assessment. First of all, internal and external sources can be located and acquired to finance this innovation project. This good management of the budget would retain the cost within a limit and resources efficient. On the other hand, return on investment could reveal strategic and financial consequences to the organization. Also, funding requires successful risk management, exploitation of partnership and collaboration with opening the channel of communication. All these ideas offer the view of how organizations underpin their striving towards innovation, growth, and success in a dynamic and competitive economy.

Building Strategic Partnerships

The creation of strategic partnerships is an indispensable ingredient of today's corporate strategy and finds application in stimulating growth, augmenting capabilities, and fighting rough markets. Coming together with other companies to achieve aims mutually desired through complementary capabilities and mutual barriers are the objectives of a strategic partnership. In structure, these partnerships may be none other than alliances, consortiums, joint ventures, cooperatives, or some other form. This section, therefore, underlines the advantages accruing to strategic alliances, how they are built up and managed, and for what benefits such alliances may bring in to the companies entering into them. Advantages accruing from strategic alliances involve the development of innovation capabilities, pooling of resources, and opening doors to new markets. They help the firms diversify their activities to tap into geographic locations or new customer bases that as a single enterprise would be hard to reach through an alliance with other business firms. A typical example may be a technological firm forming a partnership with a local company so that it can enter the foreign market and also utilize the expertise available from the local company. Resource sharing is another major benefit with the partnership, whereby the firms can share financial resources, human, and technological because it saves on cost and is efficient. In integrating the various insights, expertise, and technologies, strategic alliances have the power to drive innovation, and the result could be a new product, service, or solution that would never be born out of either party acting unilaterally.

Strategic development in alliances involves the seeking out of a potential partner whose values and strategic objectives are in concert with those of the organization. This would necessitate an analysis of competencies, capabilities, and strategic direction within a potential partner-that is, those that would complement a company's competitive positioning and fill in resources and skill set gaps. For instance, a software development company would seek a partner firm in hardware manufacture with a view towards integrated solutions that neither would be in a position to develop on its own. Once more, here too, the market standing of the prospective partner, its reputation, as well as the degree in which these are aligned with organizational values and culture, will need to be appraised. First critical success and mutual profit partly relies on an extensive due diligence process. The second most important activity in the course of this process is to develop, with as little delay, a clear and mutually beneficial partnership agreement once the prospective partners have been identified. Now, it is important to establish in this agreement the expectations of each party concerning what roles and responsibilities it wishes to undertake. First, an Agreement in partnership should indicate scope of cooperation, financial agreement, rights to intellectual property, and performance indicators. Though these components of agreement are well-articulated, they may give room for misunderstanding and disputes. This will ensure that all parties in business stand on the same page with regard to their contribution and goals. The means of conflict resolution, risk management, and adaptation to changed circumstances should also be clearly spelled out in the contract. A well-designed contract gives, besides the basis on which a successful partnership can be built, a guide to the conduct of management and the evaluation of the relationship. Communication plays a very important role in establishing and nurturing strategic alliances. There would be gained trust, conflict resolved, and expectations set in open and honest communication. It is in regularly held meetings, updating, and feedback sessions that each partner can raise issues relevant to progress and areas of concern relating to the development of the partnership. Protocols should be used so that the lines of communication routes are well-marked, making the flow of information not only effective but also efficient. Personal relationships amongst the major players of both the companies build up the confidence.

Onset of trust leads to cooperation, and hence, it strengthens the alliance. It ensures the common objective is there, and the organizations work in the interest of each other's betterment. Secondly, they build up their relationships with the communication aspect at the fore-front. The strategic partnership requires periodic nurturing and care to maintain and develop it. Attention would first go to partnership monitoring performance against set objectives in the delivery of expected value. Areas of success and areas of development will also need to be underlined through periodic performance reviews and assessment. Indicators and metrics should be developed for measuring partnership impacts to enable tracking progress towards objectives. Each organization would lead or start to work toward the solution of problems that might come up; these would then be collectively worked upon for finding the solutions and effect the necessary change. Proactive management will ensue the alliance is a success and continue to create value into the future. Flexibility and adaptability are also ways of having an efficient strategic alliance. With each and every minute, time changes, and so does business. With time, therefore, the partnership has to change to be able to meet the various circumstances of this time. Organizations should not be rigid but must always be open to reassessing and restructuring the partnership arrangement whenever the need be because of any new information, opportunities, or challenges arising. This openness to the atmosphere changes keeps the partnership working and relevant. Suppose there is new technology or any shift in the market; sometimes readjustments of objectives or strategy will enable them to leverage such opportunities. It would, therefore, allow organizations to keep flexible and maintain the collaborations strong and relevant. Innovation and Competitive Advantage: Strategic alliances can be used to attain these, too. Similarly, the partnerships that bring unique insight, advanced technology, or market know-how at times may drive the creation of new products and services or even business models. Innovation-driven partnerships are based mostly on common R and D, shared IP, or co-creation of something new. Such partnership provides resources to the company in terms of market know-how, and to the institution in terms of scientific knowledge. Innovation and creative cultures brought forth through partnership make for companies to better enjoy competitive advantages and accelerate their growth.

It calls for the creation and management of strategic partnerships in mitigation of various risks and challenges arising that range from rivalry between partners, through different cultures of the corporations to competitive goals. Risks in any partnership, when identified early and mitigated, ensure meager conflict with a guarantee of the success of the collaboration in the long run. Examples of such risk management techniques include standards of decision-making, procedures of conflict resolution, routine risk assessments. This will enable the team through the lines of communication to ascertain that all are after the same goal and iron out problems and issues. Strategic alliances in a nutshell are one of the major strategies for those enterprises that would like to enhance their capabilities, market share, and technological innovation. Some major advantages of strategic alliances include shared resources, innovation by way of cooperation, and new markets. Core elements that make for a successful partnership include choosing appropriate partners, establishing clear codes of conduct, continuous communication, and proactivity in managing the relationships. Additionally, there is a need for risk monitoring, flexibility, and adaptation. To that end, the organizations in today's competitive business world set their bases to win in the longer term and reach objectives with much greater successes by leveraging expertise and resources from strategic partners.

Monitoring and Adjusting Your Roadmap

What needs to be done is that the strategic plan should be duly observed, followed, and modified as required en-route so that the organization on whose behalf the strategic planning is done stays on target in view of a constantly changing situation. A roadmap is a type of strategic plan showing the route to achieve objectives. The nature of the market movements, technical advances, and changes within the organization contributes to making that initial plan an open-ended one, really. For that reason, monitoring the roadmap and making changes should be a continuous process to stay on track regarding strategic goals. Monitoring usually consists of roadmaps tracking their respective milestones and KPIs. Data on financial metrics, project timing, resource deployment, and performance results need to be up to date and collected from integrated systems. A company will, therefore, be in a position to constantly access information by which it measures its adherence to the roadmap and any deviation from it. If, for instance, any project falls off schedule, the monitoring data will show whether it is because of congestion in resources or delays due to unforeseen bottlenecks. These help the organization take early measures to overcome or minimize them before they blow out into proportion into serious ones. Strategies and activities of the roadmap are monitored regarding their effectiveness. It shall include the degree to which strategies achieve goals and realize desired results. Market entry, in this case of a new market, shall be considered: taking a look into market penetration, acquiring customers as well as increasing revenues. These results shall then be taken into consideration by the organizations to determine if the strategy is yielding any results or if it needs revision. It shall be ensured that the resources were put to work efficiently and that meaningful progress was made to realize the set goals. Results studied and the plan adjusted-that is what strategic management is. It basically means that when plan deviations arise, organizations need to make a change in order to get back in the right direction. A time deadline extension in case of addition of resources or some other strategy is appropriate to take place. This is where the company can increase the time frame, enhance the budget, or change the scope to resolve delays of a new product development project. This change shall be done after thorough examination and understanding of the effect such change may bring to the goals. Effective changes keep the roadmap fresh and enable the company to realize its strategic objectives.

The roadmap would thus need flexibility for adjustment. Companies must bend to the reality that the business world is never at rest. The relevant technology advance, market fluctuation, and competitive challenge will affect roadmap relevancy and efficiency. If one competitor introduces disruptive technology, for example, a firm may have to change its road map; this may also be the case with increasing R&D, forming new partnerships, or even in changes of marketing approaches. Adaptation can help an organization overcome uncertainties and create real opportunities. This could only be the case with the involvement of stakeholders in monitoring and making necessary changes. Changes can factor in suggestions and comments from employees, customers, partners, and investors. Customer feedback may point toward needs and preferences that have shifted and which the company has not cared for, for which development and marketing adjustments shall be needed. Such processes ensure stakeholder involvement that, in turn, nurtures a sense of ownership and alignment with improvements required. In periods of change, effective communication manages expectations with the stakeholders.

Of course, this requires frequent reviewing and updating of the roadmap to work. The reviews may be quarterly or annual in nature, assess progress, and adjustments therein. Such reviews are supposed to assess the roadmap against the initial plan, noting gaps and improvements. Organizations are also to take into consideration market developments, or those concerning the industry, which may affect the strategy. Reviewing and updating their plan allows companies to stay current regarding their goals and conditions. Utilizing continuous improvement in addition to monitoring and adjustment can help to add value to the road map through continued pursuit in enhancing procedures and methods for improved results. Organizations encourage learning through trial and error by using feedback to alter growth in the organization, investigating plans that are not performing as intended, and researching alternatives for those plans. Continuous improvement on the part of organizations should enable them to adapt to shifting conditions and raise the level of results.

It can also assist in monitoring and changing the roadmap. That can be possible using robust analytics, data visualization, and project management software that provides real-time performance updates. That way, the company is able to monitor KPIs, spot patterns in it, and do some analysis of the data. Technology facilitates better team communication and collaboration. It accelerates the pace of decision modification and making. Technology enhances the scale of accuracy, speed, and efficiency of monitoring and adjustment. While adjusting the roadmap, both short-term and long-term goals are to be targeted in a balanced way. In other words, it means balancing the short-term challenges and opportunities against the long-term strategic objectives of the organizations. Adjustments are to be made for the success of both in the short and long run. This means that a business making some change in the short run just to get out of a pressing problem, for example, should not come at the cost of its long-term goals. It will keep the balance going with the roadmap reflecting the strategic objective, and the company growing in a sustainable manner.

Put differently, strategic management is monitoring and reviewing the roadmap to ensure that businesses are on course and, as such, can easily be adapted. Monitoring will entail tracking progress done, methods applied, and performance reviews. All adjustments must be highly informed by close deviation analysis. Flexibility in adapting to new developments is key. Consulting stakeholders, reviewing, and improvement unceasingly could add to the efficacy of the plans. It also addresses how monitoring and modification practices are supported through technology, while striking a balance between short-run goals versus long-run goals. Such practices will keep the organization on the right track to relevance by prevailing over uncertainty and realization of strategic objectives in a dynamic business environment.

CHAPTER V

Innovation and Real-World Applications

Innovation in Retail

Innovation is everywhere nowadays in the fiercely competitive, fast-moving retail markets. This means there exists a need for innovation from the retailers to keep pace with the ever-changing expectations of the consumers regarding customer experience and stay competitive with others present in the market. The next section discusses the retail innovation in current trends and the technologies in use, along with how these might engage customers and affect operational efficiency.

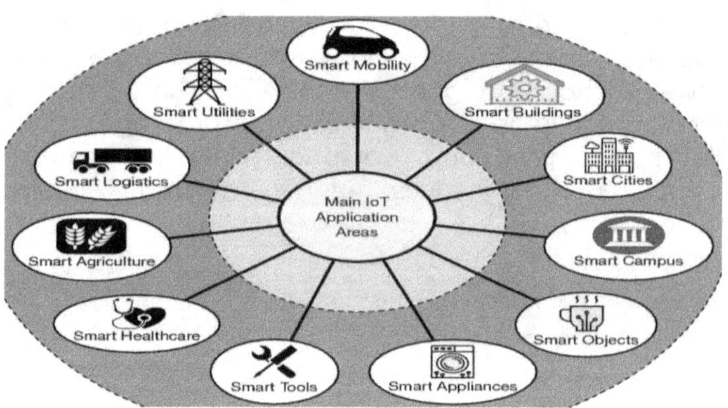

Therefore, the retail innovations have been driven by consumption behavior. The good news is that consumer preference is increasingly for shopping on mobile and online, leveraging the benefits accruing from the developments in the use of digital technology. Given this new set of preferences, digital transformation has become inevitable for retailers. E-commerce platforms, mobile applications, and omnichannel are cardinal to these. E-commerce brings convenience and more products. Mobile applications make buying easy with recommendations based on personal preference, faster options of paying, and real-time notifications. Omnichannel methods guarantee seamlessness in shifts between online and offline shops. Data-driven decision-making and personalization remain one of the biggest retail breakthroughs. Big data helps the retailer understand their customer's behavior, preference, and buying habits. The same information can be used by merchandisers to personalize marketing and product recommendations, making the inventory management personal. This can also allow a business to predict what future products will be bestsellers and whether the inventory should be stockpiled. Data-driven personalization tends to amaze customers and elicit brand loyalty, with relevant product recommendations and benefits targeted at them.

AI and machine learning have revolutionized the retail industry. They achieve it by automating retail inventory and customer service. Alongside, AI-driven chatbots reach customer inquiries round the clock to add efficiency and satisfaction. Thirdly, keeping consideration of big volumes of data, the machine learning system carries out demand estimates and fraud transaction spotting. Automate similar types of routine works through meaningful insights extracted. AI and machine learning enable the retailer to pay more attention to the adherence of his core goals and the optimization of operational performances. Other developing retail technologies are AR and VR. They bridge the gap between the worlds of physical and digital retail. For example, such AR apps would allow a buyer to see what merchandise would look like in their home-if they were to buy it. It allows making even better decisions and hence reduces returns. Through VR making, for instance, a simulation of a shop environment wherein buyers would get the opportunity to peruse and manipulate products. Such shopping experiences, though, are made more valuable through the new ways in which retailers would reach out to customers and, in turn, competitively meet other people. Stores innovate in-store.

Technology brought in the notion of smart brick-and-mortar stores, which means immersive retail. Smart retailers create personalized, interactive shopping experiences by deploying sensors and digital displays amongst other IoT devices. Smart mirrors may provide styling suggestions to complete a fit-or even allow a shopper to virtually try on an outfit. Experiential retail makes the store experience far beyond buying. Examples include interactive, hands-on, out-of-the-box product demos and eclectic in-store events. Moreover, experiential retail will also attract customers and create loyalty to brands if the shopping experience is singular and addictive. Sustainability and ethics are two other drivers of retail innovation. Whereas consumers are increasingly sensitive to environmental and social issues-for example-it is expected that retailers will further embed sustainable processes and offer merchandise that is friendly to the environment. It involves new ideas such as sustainable materials, ethical sources, and a circular economy. The big retailers started to shift into using recycled packaging or the 'take-back' program to recycle merchandise. Such initiatives would, therefore, meet customers' concerns about and reductions in environmental impact from merchants to improve brand reputation. Innovation in retail also covers technology-enabled supply chain management.

So much more supply chain transparency, efficiency, and security go on building blockchain, IoT, and advanced analytics. Blockchain technology allows items to be traced in a more secure and transparent way from the time of manufacturing to delivery, thus reducing fraud and increasing traceability. IoT devices can detect temperature and humidity during transport of products to preserve product storage and handling. Advanced analytics will then be done to predict demand, manage inventories, and detect upsets to enhance the performance of the supply chain. Advanced technologies such as these stand a chance of enabling retailers to improve the performance of the supply chains and, as such, deliver at speed. Apart from changes brought forth by technology, retail is changing because of social commerce. The products are sold with the help of social networking sites; the customers are also engaged in selling through the same. Social Commerce develops revenues and brand awareness through the use of social networks. Through social media, retailers can expose their merchandise, make focused advertisements, and enable the purchase through integrated shopping abilities. Social commerce would have allowed retailers to acquire newer customers, build trust, and develop influencer marketing much better by creating user-generated content. In retail, the pace of innovation has picked up with the COVID-19 pandemic and very much emphasizes the need for flexibility and agility.

Retailers will be in a position to make changes in online plans for sales, contactless payment, and enhancement in shop safety with new developments sooner. We are aware of how this matters to an adaptable approach in the case of disruption management and comprehension of new opportunities. What, at one time, was a matter of a choice in the innovative solutions area, turns out to be irrevocably something indispensable to life and success within the fast changes' environment. Finally, retail innovation is indispensable for the view towards competitiveness and satisfaction of consumer needs. The race never stops to find ways to further digital transformation, data-driven personalization, AI, AR, and VR for advancing customer experience and operational efficiencies. Innovation today is increasingly driven by sustainability and ethics-reflecting the increasing social responsibilities of retail. This demands that companies be open to new ideas and agile if they are to succeed in such a challenging, evolved retail environment. Innovation can allow the retailer to accept changes for growth and add value to customers and stakeholders.

Innovation in Healthcare

Health innovation transforms the delivery of medical services, enhances treatment, and simplifies health care to ensure better outcomes for patients. Innovation is supportive of problem-solving and enhancement of treatment while developing new health opportunities in light of rapid development in technology and changing health systems. Various aspects describe healthcare innovation, which includes technology, data use, personalized medicine, care to patients, and efficiency in systems. Integration of healthcare with advanced technologies is one of the huge innovations. Examples of digital health technologies that transform the delivery and management of healthcare include telemedicine and wearable health devices coupled with electronic health records. Telemedicine allows patients to consult a doctor over video conferencing and other technologies. Such technologies have greatly improved access to care in remote or otherwise underserved areas. It has also been paramount in the occurrence of certain emergencies, such as the COVID-19 pandemic, since there are reduced in-person visits, thus reducing infections.

EHRs revolutionized how patient information was managed and accessed. Digitization of records has allowed health professionals to access the instant sharing of information about patients; therefore, coordination can be swift and efficient. EHR enhances communication amongst providers, reduces errors, and allows consistency in care with an informed patient. Moreover,

EHRs enable healthcare organizations to analyze large volumes of data for better results in patient outcomes and the delivery of health care. Other health innovations include activity trackers, smartwatches, and continuous glucose monitoring. These devices track heart rate, physical activity, and glucose in real-time, providing a plethora of health information. Wearable devices facilitate patient self-management and provide the physician with the opportunity for remote monitoring of the patient. Continuous monitoring can allow timely identification of health risks, customization of treatment approaches, and improvement in the management of chronic diseases.

Another more important development in health is the application of big data analytics. As large-scale data from EHRs, clinical trials, and patient surveys get analyzed, healthcare outcomes keep improving. It would be on predictive analytics that patterns and trends emanate from the coming data to forecast the demand from the patients towards the prevention of poor outcomes. It allows healthcare professionals to analyze patient data on the appropriateness of therapies and resources to optimize resource allocation. Big data contributes to evidence-based procedures and to decision-making for therapies. Personalized medicine is very innovative and tailored according to the particular quality in each patient. These advances in genomics and biotechnology help doctors understand better how variations in genes of a specific individual determine how they react to a certain medicine and how susceptible one is to diseases. The basis for personalized medicine treatment programs includes genetic information, lifestyle, and environmental data for each particular individual. By doing so, this maximizes the therapeutic efficacy while minimizing adverse effects. The application of personalized medicine is more precise in terms of care about a single patient than a one-size-fits-all concept.

Innovative health concerns new medical treatments and remedies. Pharmaceutical, biotechnology, and medical device innovations have provided new solutions to hitherto unmet medical needs. Targeted medicines and immunotherapies have raised the standard of care in cancer treatment with fewer toxicities. Where diseased tissues and organs have not been repairable, either alone or in combination, regenerative medicine innovations like stem cell therapy and tissue engineering may repair or replace diseased tissues and organs. Taken together, these can offer a sea change in the results and quality of life for patients with the most complex health. AI and machine learning are also being implemented in the field of health. AI algorithms will help diagnose diseases and other abnormalities in medical pictures, such as X-rays and MRI. Machine learning algorithms will predict patient outcomes through treatments, referring, and underlining risks from past data. AI can be used to help with scheduling and billing services, further streamlining operations at hospitals. AI can improve clinical and operational healthcare by automating routine tasks and offering better analytics.

Innovation in health carries lots of advantages, but it has created its own disadvantages, too. For the digital technologies of health and data analytics, privacy and security are of utmost import-protection of patient data against illegal access and cyberattacks will contribute to the building of trust and satisfaction of legislation. Planning and coordination will definitely be required for integrating new technologies into healthcare systems. Some considerations to be made by a healthcare business before the deployment of an innovative solution are the levels of interoperability, training of staff, and expenditure thereof. Others are the issue of equity in access to medical innovations; technology can expand access to care and quality, but digital health disparities in tools and resources continue to drive the gaps. The innovations must be able to serve all patients regardless of socioeconomic backgrounds, location, or any other consideration. There is the need for activities related to Targeted health care inclusiveness and accessibility in order to close the gap.

The adoption of innovation in health requires a cultural change. While adopting newer technologies, the changing of habits and mindsets is quite common. For innovation, new ways of working need to be kept in focus with regard to patients. The collaboration of technology developers, health professionals, and politicians must be in tune with one another while creating innovation and implementing newer ideas into clinical practice. Innovation in the health sector means innovation of medical practice and patient care, improvement in the system. Telemedicine, EHRs, and wearables have reworked the scale of healthcare management. Big data and personalized medicine represent two ways in which patient outcomes can be improved through adjusting therapies. Development in medicine, AI, and machine learning is a peek at how innovation is translated and will be used to transform healthcare. The realization of full potential by health innovations would call for a consideration of privacy, access, and cultural changes. The health care industry will go forth in making quality and effective care available for all by embracing such advances and their challenges.

Innovation in Finance

Financial innovation has made the ecosystem of financial services, consumption, and regulation-a very different kettle of fish. Some major reasons for bringing such drastic change into the world of finance include advanced integrations of technology, emerging business models, and shifts in consumer expectations. In this section, I will discuss three major spheres of innovation in finance: digital transformation, finance technology advances, and their effect on traditional banking and investment practices.

Most of all, digitization is one of the most important innovations in finance. The rapid development of digital banking and mobile solutions to pay really revolutionized the way people handle their finances. Since then, traditional banks also modernized with mobile applications and an online platform where customers can easily transact, check their balance, and conduct financial services anywhere. These digital facilities provide convenience and efficiency previously unavailable, reducing most of the compulsion to visit a bank branch physically. Therefore, the power of being able to undertake financial transactions on the move has empowered consumers toward better money management, and it has opened up new avenues for ensuring financial inclusion.

This has seen an application of technology in the dispensation of innovative financial services, with the emergence of big players in the financial sector, so-called fintech companies. These have foisted a number of disrupting solutions on everything from peer-to-peer lending platforms to robo-advisors, hosting cryptocurrency exchanges, and blockchains. Peer-to-peer lending platforms connect borrowers directly with investors, bypassing the traditional channel through financial intermediaries and, in the process, often offer superior rates for the borrowers and more attractive returns for the investor. Robo-advisors have made financial planning more accessible and affordable through automated investment advice and portfolio management due to algorithms. First of all, cryptocurrencies and blockchain introduce new ways of transacting and asset management, which shakes conventional financial systems, thus paving the way for DeFi.

Most importantly, blockchain technology is hyped as the term itself implies disruption in how many segments in finance will ever work. In a nutshell, it is a distributed ledger whose primary function is recording transactions in a way that is secure and transparent. It empowers secure and rapid cross-border payments with minimal risks of fraud while concurrently improving the accuracy of financial records. Other than in the case of payment, blockchain technology can also be applied to smart contracts, which are self-executable agreements whereby terms are directly written in lines of code. Smart contracts automated cumbersome processes and transactions, hence, in most cases, avoiding the need for intermediaries; instead, they made this effective.

However, big data and AI have accelerated this stride of innovation in the financial industry even further. While AI and machine learning continue to grow, their application to finance through analysis by financial institutions through huge reams of data increasingly comport customer behavior, market trends, and risk management. With the ability to find patterns and anomalies in economic data, AI algorithms have more accurate fraud detection and risk assessments. Such machine learning models easily make a forecast of future market movements and optimize trading strategy, hence giving an edge in investment decision-making over competitors. Driven by AI, chatbots and virtual assistants raise customer service improvement through instantaneous support and personalized recommendations.

The next fast-growing field of innovation in the financial world is regulatory technology, shortly known as RegTech. Regtech solutions apply the use of technology to simplify regulatory compliance and lighten the burden of regulatory reporting. These solutions tap into data analytics, automation, and AI in carrying out the needed transaction monitoring, detection of compliance events, and reporting. While enabling the financial institution to meet various requirements set up by regulatory bodies with much greater efficiency, it would also reduce the risk of regulatory breaches and related fines. Other developments within the financial world concern the new financial products and services developed. Examples include such things as sustainable finance, which reflects a growing focus on environmental, social, and governance issues. Meanwhile, new financial instruments, such as green bonds or socially responsible investment funds, enable private investors to make their portfolios in line with their values and, at the same time, be contributors to sustainable projects. Besides, the added integration of financial services with other major sectors like health and education opens up new frontiers for financial inclusions and personalized services.

While there are numerous benefits to innovation finance, there are also a number of concerns and considerations. The rapid rate of technological change means that financial institutions must be able to adapt to new investments in technologies constantly. In a world where there are cyber threats and other data breaches, cybersecurity and the privacy of digital deals and personal information are very important. In addition, new challenges that appeared when new technologies were implemented included regulatory and compliance issues. In fact, changes that FIs have to go through in terms of regulatory frameworks so that innovative solutions can meet the legality required. Innovations in finance differ in ways of structuring novelty in technologies, business models, and financial products. Digitization of financial services, development and growth of Fin-tech and Blockchain, and integration of AI and Big Data replace ways in which financial services are produced and consumed. Whereas innovation provides a host of opportunities, it also points toward challenges with respect to security, compliance, and adaptation. In the future, innovation will remain adopted within the financial sector in overcoming various challenges, but it will be at the heart of encouraging more growth in this sector and key to enhancing value for consumers and businesses.

Innovation in Manufacturing

Manufacturing innovation reached a point where, from then on, the drivers were to be essentially efficiency, high-quality products, and competitive advantage. The manufacturing sector continuously goes through changes as new developments crop up in technology and methodology. This section intends to discuss some major innovations that have happened and are happening within manufacturing, including automation, additive manufacturing, IoT, and sustainable practices, in terms of how these new developments affect the face of manufacturing. Instead, the concept of manufacturing innovation has brought automation to the fore that has changed a lot in the production process, hence contributing to more efficiencies. Greater integration of robotics and automated machinery is giving the manufacturer more ability to increase the speed of production, reduce labor costs, and ensure much greater precision in operations. Robots conduct repetitive work with unparalleled consistency, something very important in the quality of products and reducing the risk of human error. Besides, automation allows flexibility in production because such systems can be reconfigured for the handling of varied products or changes in demand. This trend is further reflected in the development and growing adoption of collaborative robots-that is to say, robots-that work alongside human operators, allowing for a closer integration with the collaboration between human and machine on the factory floor.

Additive manufacturing, better known under its popular designation of 3D printing, constitutes yet another disruptive innovation in manufacturing. Unlike the traditional subtractive manufacturing methods, where material is being cut from a block, additive manufacturing builds objects layer by layer from digital models. In other words, it offers increased geometrical complexity, custom parts, and rapid prototyping. Of particular value, the prototyping and fabrication of complex parts through 3D printing are faster and less costly. Applications include most industries, such as aerospace, automotive, and health-where customized parts and precision will be most important. It would reduce dependence on large inventories and long lead times associated in general with high-quality, low-volume components manufacturing to order.

Thus, IoT has surely opened a new vista in manufacturing characterized by connectivity and data-driven insights into operations. IoT is at least an integrated network of sensors embedded in devices and machines that can connect through a network to gather and analyze data in real time. It allows manufacturers to maintain monitoring of performance, production metrics, and maintenance forecasts via connected machinery and systems. IoT analytics serve as the drive towards actionable insight into operational efficiency, and it supports data-driven decisions as well as process optimization. A good example would be predictive maintenance, where IoT provides the required warning of an impending failure that prevents downtime and reduces disruption to production. Improvement and quality control also rely on gathering and analyzing information from different sources.

Manufacturing innovation is ever-increasingly being driven by considerations of sustainability and environmental concern. The result of this is the increase in the pace of those industrial practices and technologies that assure minimal environmental impact, together with strongly efficient resource use. Inventions relating to energy-saving machinery keep cropping up; waste-reducing methods keep cropping up, and so do sustainable materials. It has been observed that the companies do find means towards carbon reduction when there is the use of closed-loop systems, where material is recycled as well as reduced in terms of waste. Moreover, the green manufacturing practices, which include renewable energy usage along with water consumption reduction, have gained increased momentum. Moreover, the transition towards sustainable manufacturing will pay in the long run, not only because regulatory requirements will necessitate it, but also because consumers expect it and it guarantees efficiency with fewer costs.

New material and technology development is another key driver of innovation. The development of newer materials like composite materials and nanomaterials opened up wider vistas for the manufacturing of high-performance products. These are, in fact the superior materials, such that they are strong, light, and durable. For innovative improvements in the ways of manufacture allowed such precision machining and state-of-the-art welding techniques whereby complex and quality components could be manufactured. Along with other digital technologies like CAD and CAM, this becomes even more articulate and efficient.

Where most of the advantages of innovation exist, there remain a few challenges to be overcome within manufacturing. Most of these state-of-the-art technologies require huge investments in their adoption on the production floor, rather expensive in respect of infrastructural investments, training, and maintenance. There are scaling considerations-things like scope-for technologies within current systems and processes. Furthermore, cybersecurity becomes a high concern while manufacturing gets more and more connected; thus, the possibility of cyber threats and data breaches puts into question operational integrity. Therefore, manufacturing innovation through increased efficiency, quality improvement of products, and sustainability drives an industrial transformation. The drivers that have brought massive changes in the ways of production in terms of processes and capabilities include automation, additive manufacturing, IoT, and advanced materials. Innovations within these aspects come with several challenges that relate to investment, integration, and cybersecurity. With innovation, or quite simply with the care of all challenges that accompany innovation, the manufacturing industry always reinvents itself to make its future growth and competitive advantage possible in the global market.

Synthesizing Lessons Across Industries

Cross-industry synthesis of lessons is one of those key practices that drive continuous innovation and improvement by taking ideas and strategies from one industry to another. Accelerating problem-solving and cross-pollination enriches the adaptiveness and resiliency of organizations. These would then lead an organization to adopt the best practices, find new ways, and, lastly, come up with better results for research that studies how different sectors respond to common challenges and opportunities. The section below attempts to establish reasons as to why synthesis across industries is necessary, examples of successful cases when an application across the industry worked, and, in turn, the benefits and challenges that happen when this practice is carried out. Synthesizing experiences across industries holds one important reason: finding an innovative solution for common problems may be quite great. Each sector differs in its own particular set of problems. Yet, it is obvious that many of those problems represent variants of other issues that share similar causes. However, the healthcare vertical faces unique challenges in managing patients, and operational efficiency, inventory management, and customer experience are areas of concern for many of their respective retail industries.

Knowing how analytics and predictive modeling achieve retail inventory optimization, similar techniques can be applied to extend scheduling and resource allocation to healthcare providers. Similarly, food and beverage manufacturing can learn some supply chain management lessons that could streamline logistics and distribution. This transfer of technology and associated logistics not only provides better solutions but also accelerates the pace whereby new strategies are developed and put into practice.

Indeed, one of the striking examples of cross-industry learning is around the use of technology. Financial services have applied advanced data analytics and algorithmic trading to optimize investment strategies and risk management for decades, and surprisingly, much of the best practices and technologies in use have translated quite successfully to the healthcare sector in terms of predictive analytics of patient care. For example, machine learning algorithms previously used to predict financials are finding new applications in predicting patient outcomes and developing treatment plans that are best suited for the individual. Blockchain technology has also been explored for healthcare and supply chain management applications that offer security and transparency when recording information. These examples serve to illustrate how the technological advances of one industry can be harnessed to help another rise to a challenge with efficiencies and improved results. Other areas in which such cross-industry syntheses have proven their worth are in the realm of customer experience and service delivery-the personal touch, the essence of the tourism business, caters to the needs of the guests. Retailers, too, have increasingly mirrored this by taking customer data to personalize marketing, create experiences in-store, and make personalized product recommendations. Indeed, it is this very ethos that has been formulated and fine-tuned in the process of building memories and experiences within the hospitality industry, harnessed here within retail strategies in the pursuit of enhanced customer engagement and loyalty. The lessons from the seamless, intuitive online services provided by technology companies taught financial services and other industries how to design online platforms and communicate with their customers.

In closing, cross-industry learning is a potent strategy for fostering innovation, problem-solving, and organizational performance. Businesses allow finding new ways to smoothen operation processes and develop better products and services by applying insights and strategies from one sector to another. Cross-industry learning has tried and worked well in terms of technology applications, customer experience strategies, and product development practices. If this practice is to be truly useful, each obstacle in adapting lessons within disparate contexts and overcoming resistance to change must be addressed. Embracing cross-industry synthesis cultivates innovation that enables the organization to maintain a competitive advantage, being more responsive to emerging market needs.

CONCLUSION

In a nutshell, from the book "Harnessing Innovation: Driving Change in a Digital Age: Embracing Technology for Business Success," what adds up is that probably the only viable route to success in the modern world remains to embrace the dynamism between innovation and technology.

In a volatile, changing world, indeed, the new normal-adaptability and innovation have ceased to be mere options but an intrinsic ingredient of survival and further growth. These are the two major promoters of innovation in this book: leadership leading from the front and technology for use as a strategic value enabler to assist business change.

It is something that cannot be one-time; ongoing commitment is needed to build an enabling culture that is innovative, nimble, and future-ready. They will, therefore, by learning from case studies in their natural habitat and through the execution of strategies discussed here variously, place themselves in a position to lead change in the marketplace rather than react to it. Only such a future truly belongs to those who can harness the power of innovation to unlock new possibilities to redefine industries.

Reality is the most successful organizations innately integrate innovation into their DNA. The challenges and opportunities brought about by the digital age require an open mind, a strategic frame of mind, and, above all, an insatiable drive for innovation. The tools and learnings from this book are your roadmap to bring that vision into being.